A GUIDE TO ESSEX CHURCHES

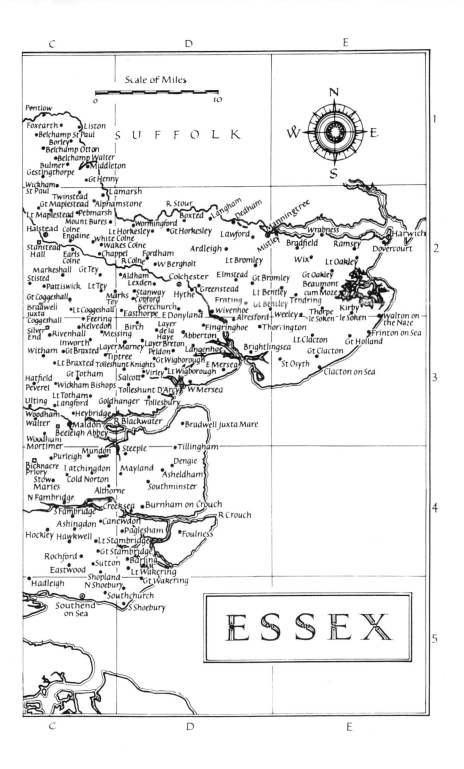

C   D   E

Scale of Miles

0   10

N
W   E
S

1

Pentlow
Foxearth •
• Liston
• Belchamp St Paul
Borley •
• Belchamp Otton
• Belchamp Walter
Bulmer • • Middleton
Gestingthorpe •
• Gt Henny
Wickham
St Paul
Twinstead • Lamarsh
Gt Maplestead Alphamstone
Lt Maplestead • Pebmarsh
Mount Bures •
Halstead Colne
Engaine
White Colne
• Wakes Colne
Stansted
Hall Earls • Chappel Fordham
Colne
Markeshall Gt Tey
Stisted
• Pattiswick Lt Tey
Gt Coggeshall
Bradwell
juxta • Lt Coggeshall
Coggeshall
Silver • Feering
End • Rivenhall • Kelvedon
Inworth
Witham • Gt Braxted
• Lt Braxted
Hatfield Gt Totham
Peverel • Wickham Bishops
Lt Totham
Ulting Langford
Woodham • Heybridge
Walter
Woodham
Mortimer
• Purleigh
Bicknacre
Priory Latchingdon
Stow • Cold Norton
Maries
Althorne
N Fambridge
S Fambridge
Ashingdon • Canewdon
Hockley Hawkwell
• Lt Stambridge
Rochford • • Gt Stambridge
Eastwood • Sutton • Barling
Shopland • Lt Wakering
Hadleigh N Shoebury • Gt Wakering
• Southchurch
Southend • S Shoebury
on Sea

SUFFOLK

R Stour
Boxted Langham Dedham
Wormingford
Lt Horkesley • Gt Horkesley Lawford
Ardleigh
R Colne • W Bergholt
Aldham Colchester Elmstead
Lexden
Marks Stanway Greenstead
Tey Copford Hythe
Berechurch Frating
• Easthorpe E Donyland Wivenhoe
Birch Layer Alresford
de la • Fingringhoe
Messing Haye Abberton • Thorrington
Layer Marney Layer Breton
Tiptree Peldon Langenhoe
Tolleshunt Knights • Gt Wigborough E Mersea
• Virley • Lt Wigborough
Salcott
Tolleshunt D'Arcy • W Mersea
Goldhanger Tollesbury
R Blackwater
Maldon • Bradwell juxta Mare
Beeleigh Abbey
Mundon • Steeple • Tillingham
Dengie
Mayland •
• Asheldham
Southminster
Creeksea • Burnham on Crouch
R Crouch
Paglesham
• Foulness

Manningtree
Mistley Wrabness
Bradfield Ramsey Harwich
Wix • Lt Oakley Dovercourt
Gt Bromley Gt Oakley
Lt Bentley Beaumont
cum Moze
Gt Bentley Tendring
Weeley Thorpe Kirby
le Soken le Soken Walton on
• Thorrington the Naze
Lt Clacton Frinton on Sea
Gt Holland
Brightlingsea
Gt Clacton
St Osyth
Clacton on Sea

2

3

4

E S S E X

5

C   D   E

Dedham. Soffit of Galilee beneath the tower, c.1519.

A GUIDE TO ESSEX CHURCHES

Edited by Christopher Starr with an introduction by Sir William Addison and an epilogue by the Bishop of Chelmsford.

Published by

The Essex Churches Support Trust
1980

ISBN 0 907281 00 1

Printed by Hart-Talbot Limited,
Shirehill Industrial Estate, Saffron Walden, Essex
for the Essex Churches Support Trust.

CONTENTS

Cover: South Hanningfield church, door at *Castle Hedingham* by Lois Bull

INTRODUCTION

Sir William Addison

Name any English county to an experienced student of churches and a typical landscape, with a church built in a local style will immediately be visualised. If the county named is Sussex, the church may be either a Saxon shepherds' church on the Downs or an ironmaster's church in the Weald; if it is Somerset, it may be one of the Mendip churches built in a style derived from the ornate architecture of Wells Cathedral, one in the Quantock villages built by the masons from Taunton or Glastonbury, or one on Exmoor built by local masons in the plainer styles that continue into Devon. Practically all the clearly defined styles that are characteristic of their counties can be explained in terms of the stone of which they are built and the people who built them. The sources of building styles in Essex are more complex. Although the county became pre-eminent in the use of brick and timber in its churches, it is doubtful whether there is a style that is exclusively characteristic of it. Its few large churches would not qualify. *Waltham Abbey* is unique in Essex. Kentish styles cross the Thames into the south of the county, the three great churches at *Dedham, Thaxted,* and *Saffron Walden* are East Anglian in style. The general run of ancient churches in Essex - and there are hundreds of them - are fascinating medleys.

One reason for this is the unusually large number of overseas influences that can be traced in them. Another is that apart from the nodules of limestone called septaria and the hard chalk called clunch, Essex has no local stone to give consistent character to its churches. This meant that the builders, most of whom were estate masons, had to make what use they could of stones raked from the fields or deposits dredged from the streams, which when embedded in mortar have proved more durable than many professionally worked sandstones. A county's character, like a child's, is formed early, and research is increasingly showing that long before historical records began, indigenous skills in the use of this jumble of rubble, timber, and flint for building were acquired by natives who had survived successive invasions in the forests of mid-Essex and along the coastal fringe.

A third explanation is found in the distinctive character that developed in the county's churchmanship and the kind of buildings it favoured for worship. The historical record begins with Cedd's two minsters built on fortified sites at *Bradwell-on-Sea* and *Tilbury,* probably because they had good communications and material at hand for building. From Bradwell the Gospel was carried to *Canewdon,* another fortified site, and forerunners of the parish system were established at *Southminster* for the south-east of the Saxon kingdom and *Upminster* for the south. In the development of parishes from minsters, Essex is comparable with Dorset in that in both of them, minsters were mission centres from which large areas were evangelized with no other object than to meet the spiritual needs of the people. In Dorset these became market towns with "Minster" incorporated in their place-names, in which ecclesiastical and secular life developed together. Pastoral letters in English, along with paraphrases of parts of the Bible, were circulated from Cerne Abbey for the education of the people. In short, the Scriptures and moral welfare rather than the liturgy determined the character of the county's churchmanship.

This reconciling of secular and spiritual needs had started in Essex with the rebuilding of Saxon churches in Norman style by lords of manors shortly after the Conquest. Later these same lords of manors endowed upwards of fifty religious houses, most of which were of Augustinian canons whose vocation did not cut them off from the World. The wealthiest was *Waltham Abbey,* and the simplicity of style still seen in the medieval churches of the West Essex villages, many of which were staffed from Waltham, is evidence of the abbey's practical churchmanship. There were three Cistercian houses in Essex; but the Cistercians were equally simple in their building styles. Only where de Vere influence was strong, as at *Castle Hedingham, Earls*

Colne, and *Hatfield Broad Oak* do we get churches built in the grand style associated with the ambitious Benedictines. Nowhere in Essex was there the kind of autocratic rule exercised by the proud abbot of St Edmundsbury in Suffolk. In Essex the traditional link was between the church and the manor house.

The way in which this link was strengthened after the Dissolution is well illustrated in the county's response to a national call made in 1569 for all J.P.s to observe the new Order and persuade their tenants to do likewise. Sixty Essex J.P.s signed a declaration of loyalty at a meeting held at Chelmsford on the 25th November in that year, and many of their descendants have continued to show their loyalty by acting as rector's warden. Archdeaconry records add their testimony in such entries as the one for *Great Chesterford* under date 1587 which reads: "To make a pewe for the minister in the body of the church to read Divine Service". Later again, when most of the beneficed clergymen sat on the county Bench, Christianity became more than ever a practical affair in Essex—so much so that when the custom of appointing clergy to the Commission of the Peace was suspended one of them wrote asking how he could be expected to preach morality effectively from the pulpit on Sunday if he could not reinforce it from the Bench on Monday.

This is the tradition that gave Essex churches which, although few may be great architectural monuments, all are faithful records of the life and faith of "our fathers that begat us".

The moral for us is that these churches have been maintained for hundreds of years by the offerings of the faithful generously supplemented in rural parishes by the patron of the living, who after noticing a crack in the masonry, or evidence of rot in the timbering when he went round the pews with the collection plate on Sunday, would send the estate mason or carpenter along on the first wet day to start the necessary repairs. That is why so few parishes provided for repairs. Now it is for all of us to shoulder the responsibility of maintaining this precious heritage. I am happy as President of *Friends of Essex Churches* and a founder member to write this introduction to a most valuable series of articles explaining just what that heritage is.

CHURCH ARCHAEOLOGY

Warwick Rodwell

The history of a church begins, not with its first mention in a document or with the oldest visible elements of its architecture, but with the earliest evidence for some form of religious activity on the site. This evidence may well be buried beneath the churchyard turf, or under the floors, or encapsulated in the fabric of standing walls, perhaps hidden from view by plaster and rendering. If we are properly to understand and appreciate the histories of our cathedrals, churches and chapels, it is obviously imperative to discover when they were erected, why they were built where they are, by whom, and how they have evolved over the centuries. We may go further and ask fundamental questions such as: did a timber church precede one in masonry; did the graveyard come into existence before the church; was the site chosen because of some pre-Christian significance; and was the church erected for the use of a local lord and his family, a lay population or a monastic community?

Opportunities for investigation

There were more than 450 medieval churches and monasteries in the historic county of Essex, and in no more than a handful of instances do we know the answers to the above questions. But these vital facts are by no means lost beyond recall, and it is here that church archaeology has a tremendous role to play. As a disciplined subject it is relatively new, being essentially a development of the 1960s and '70s (not to be confused with the long tradition of antiquarian studies, which it partly embodies and supersedes). Church archaeology is concerned with the study of the whole history and topography of churches and graveyards, and with all their respective monuments, fittings and furnishings. The discipline embraces traditional studies such as local history, architectural history and art history, as well as field survey and excavation, demography and palaeopathology. Thus the archaeological investigation of a church is a highly complex and technical subject, which relies upon many separate skills in the arts and sciences.

Several large-scale projects have taken place on Essex churches in recent years (eg. at *Rivenhall, Hadstock, Asheldham, West Bergholt, St Peter's Bradwell,* and *St Giles' Colchester),* yielding substantial returns for ecclesiastical and local history. The urgency for undertaking such investigations is underlined by the ever increasing losses incurred through the processes of natural decay, redundancy, injurious restoration and wanton destruction, such as churchyard clearance.

Church origins

Evidence bearing upon Christianity in the Roman period is slowly coming to light in Essex: there are possible Christian cemeteries and structures on the south side of Colchester, a baptismal font has been excavated at Witham and various objects bearing Christian emblems have been found, such as the Chi-Rho finger-ring from Brentwood and the Alpha-Omega monogram from Wickford.

Christianity probably faded away in the mid fifth century and was not reasserted until the mission headed by St Cedd arrived in A.D. 653. New churches began to be built, and the first recorded monasteries were founded at *Bradwell-on-Sea* and *West Tilbury.* The plans of 7th-century monastic churches are distinctive and Bradwell is the only one from Essex known in detail, but it is evident that another of closely similar design is preserved in the foundations of *Prittlewell* church.

Other early Saxon churches obviously await discovery, and at least two may be suspected at *Colchester.* One is *St Helen's Chapel* which in part incorporates standing Roman walls, and the other is the hitherto unknown structure discovered in

St John's Abbey grounds in 1972. Its foundations may also incorporate Roman work. Also in Colchester, it should be noted that the nave of *Holy Trinity* church is older than the famous 10th-century tower. The reuse of Roman building materials (present in nearly one third of all medieval churches in Essex) or standing walls (as also at *St Nicholas'*, Colchester) was very widespread in the Anglo-Saxon and Norman periods. These connections are by no means all fortuitous, and the old idea that churches were often built over Roman villas (as at *Rivenhall, Alphamstone, West Mersea* and *Stansted Mountfitchet*) simply for the convenience of obtaining a ready supply of rubble is no longer acceptable.

Furthermore, there is now clear evidence that at least some churches were built on the sites of Roman or early Saxon cemeteries, and that it was the sepulchral element which provided continuity. Thus at *Colchester, St Botolph's Priory, St John's Abbey* and *St Giles' Church* are all in the main Roman cemetery areas. At *Great Chesterford* the church is probably situated in or beside a Roman and Saxon cemetery; the church at *Braintree* lies in the suburbs of the Roman town, quite possibly a cemetery area, and elsewhere Roman burial urns have been found in or adjacent to churchyards (eg. *Great Maplestead, Rivenhall* and *Mucking*).

To date, no example of a pagan religious building has been found under a church in Essex, but an association with springs and ponds is noticeable in some places. Water-bearing features of the landscape were often places of pagan worship and gathering which became absorbed into Christian ideology as 'holy wells'. In Essex the names of few holy wells have survived, but these include St Botolph's, *Hadstock*, St German's *Faulkbourne*, St Peter's *Coggeshall* and St Anne's *Colchester*.

It is important to remember that the great majority of churches were built as proprietary chapels of local lords, probably mainly in the 10th and 11th centuries, and not as places of worship for the community at large. This accounts for the fact that so many Essex churches form integral parts of manorial complexes: thus at places like *Lindsell, Little Bardfield, Dengie, Wickham St Paul* and *Little Wigborough* the church lies virtually in the grounds of the hall, perpetuating the intimate relationship which has doubtless existed for a thousand years. In certain instances one building, usually the hall, has been demolished or moved to a new site, leaving the other now isolated. At *Little Stambridge, Snoreham, Ingrave, Moze* and *Langenhoe* it is the church which has been demolished, leaving only the hall. At *Markshall* both have been destroyed In recent years.

The results of church archaeology

All investigations and observations are valuable and the information recovered from them is adding a whole new dimension to local and national history. Two examples of recent work may be mentioned.

St Mary and All Saints Rivenhall. This is a good example of a proprietary church founded in the late Saxon period in a pre-existing graveyard. Archaeological investigations (1971-78) have revealed both the history of the church and the settlement which it served, where continuity from the pre-Roman period to the present day has been demonstrated. The large Roman villa which underlies the church continued to form the nucleus of a group of inhabited buildings in the pagan Saxon period, but in the 7th century, or a little later, a new hall was built just to the north of the villa, and a Christian cemetery was established in the old villa courtyard. A chapel or mausoleum was built on the ruins of the villa, and was superseded in the 10th century by a small timber church (fig. 1.3). This was in turn replaced by an Anglo-Saxon stone-built church, most of which survives to the present day, although it was completely masked until 1972 by medieval and modern accretions.

In the later 11th century the stone church was enlarged by the addition of an apsidal sanctuary, which was then swept away by improvements in the early 14th century. Late in the same century a western tower was added, but this collapsed in 1714, and a new Georgian brick tower was erected three years later. Finally, in 1839

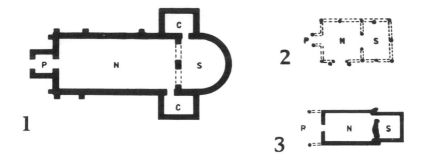

1

2

3

7

8

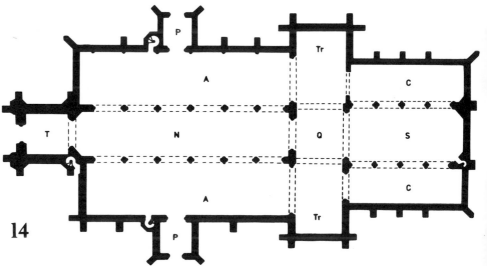

14

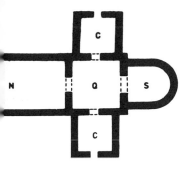

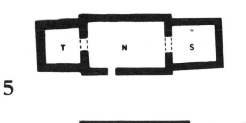

5

6

9

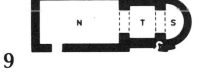

10

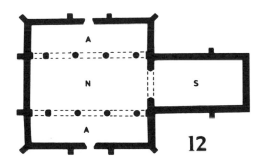

12

11

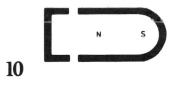

13

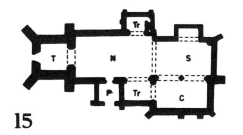

15

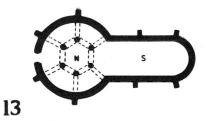

A	Aisle	C	Chapel
N	Nave	P	Porch
Q	Quire	S	Sanctuary
T	Tower	Tr	Transept

13

the whole building was given a Gothic atmosphere by adding battlements and turrets, replacing all windows and covering the walls with stucco.

St Botolph Hadstock. This cruciform minster church was excavated and studied in 1974-79. The present building was probably begun in the 9th century and overlies domestic occupation of the middle Saxon period. The plan of the church, although always cruciform, has evolved over the centuries with major changes to both the east and west ends. Originally there was probably a simple quire at the crossing (Fig. 1.4), but later a timber tower was erected here; this was replaced in the first half of the 11th century by a stone-built tower, which collapsed in the 13th century. Two hundred years later a new western tower was erected.

At Hadstock archaeology has shown that parts of the roof, four wooden window frames and the north door are all of late Anglo-Saxon workmanship. The only other known pre-conquest door in England is also in Essex, at *Buttsbury*, but that is in a poor state of preservation. Neither of these doors hangs in its original position. The log-built church at *Greensted-juxta-Ongar* is of course the best known surviving piece of Anglo-Saxon carpentry; the evidence for churches of similar construction has been found by excavation at *Rivenhall* and *Asheldham*. Two timber buildings of rather different form—probably successive churches—have been excavated at *Nazeingbury*, where they were associated with a cemetery of middle Saxon date (Fig. 1.2). Both the churches and the graveyard were abandoned and had disappeared by the medieval period.

Elsewhere in the county recent archaeological investigations have revealed many interesting and unsuspected details about the histories of churches. For example, it is clear that many more churches had apsidal chancels in the late Saxon and Norman periods, but have long ago been altered (eg. *Asheldham, Cressing, Easthorpe* and *Ingrave*). At *Asheldham*, too, there was the unexpected discovery that a tower had once existed over the chancel (Fig 1.9); this may also have been the original arrangement at *Boreham*.

By a careful study of the evidence, both above and below ground, inside and outside a church, it is becoming possible to reconstruct the original arrangements for scaffolding used by Saxon and medieval builders, to determine how many courses of stone they laid in a day, and where they stopped work and capped off the walls for the winter. Inside, it may be possible to recover evidence for patterns of medieval floor tiling, wall decorations, benches and seats, altar and font positions, and even the way people walked about in churches, as perpetuated in the wear patterns in ancient floors.

Church Plans

Archaeology has demonstrated most dramatically how churches grew and developed over the centuries. There is hardly a handful of ancient churches in Essex which remain substantially in the form in which they were first built. Some have been completely rebuilt, usually in a piecemeal fashion, and often several times over; a great many have been extended eastwards and westwards; others have had side aisles formed; and scores of porches, towers, chapels and vestries have been added. Not only may the plan of a church be composite, but so may also its elevations: new windows and doorways may have been inserted into old walls, clerestories added, roofs rebuilt and towers heightened.

Figure 1. *A selection of Essex church plans (some partially reconstructed). 1. Bradwell-on-Sea, St Peter (7th cent.); 2. Nazeingbury (timber, 9th cent.); 3. Rivenhall (timber, 10th cent.); 4. Hadstock (9th-10th cent.); 5. Little Bardfield (10th cent.); 6. Broomfield (11th cent.); 7. Colchester, St Martin (12th cent.); 8. Copford (12 cent.); 9. Asheldham (11th-12th cent.); 10. Little Tey (11th-12 cent.); 11. Little Coggeshall (13th cent.); 12. Stisted (13th cent.); 13. Little Maplestead (14th cent.); 14. Thaxted (15th cent); 15. East Horndon (15th-16th cent.).*

15a. *Rivenhall. Burial of middle Saxon date showing the early Christian rite of piling stones around the skull.*

15b. *Hadstock. Saxon nave, 14th century north transept, 15th century tower and porch, and 19th century chancel.*

16a. *Rivenhall. Recording the excavated foundations of the chancel.*

16b. *Hadstock. Excavating the Saxon floor levels inside the church.*

Not all these additions have remained to the present day, and the following may be noted amongst the deletions: the west end of the nave at *Buttsbury* and *Great Tey*; parts of the chancel at *Little Saling* and *Peldon*; the south aisle at *North Shoebury* and *East Tilbury*; a south chapel or transept at *Southminster* and part of the north transept at *St Osyth*; and the west tower at *Wimbish, Birchanger, Alphamstone*, etc. Where a parish church was once part of a monastic house only a very small fragment of the original complex usually remains standing, as at *Hatfield Peverel, Hatfield Broad Oak, Waltham Holy Cross* and *Little Dunmow*.

Finally, some ancient churches have disappeared entirely or are completely ruined, and are now just archaeological sites: such has been the fate of at least 47 in Essex. Important ruins include *Stanway All Saints, Little Birch* and *Alresford*; small fragments remain of *Virley, Markshall* and *Little Henny*; while of *Belchamp St Ethelbert* and *Thunderley* there is nothing to be seen but ploughed fields. *Thunderley*, incidentally, is the earliest recorded redundant church in Essex, having been abandoned in 1425.

THE PLANNING OF THE MEDIAEVAL CHURCH AND ITS USE.

Laurence King

Introduction

It may be stated that no country in Europe has so magnificent, so varied and so rich a collection of Parish Churches as has our own, and they thus form a most important part of our architectural heritage. Their appeal stretches far and wide and well beyond the faithful who worship weekly and, in many cases, daily within their walls. First and foremost we need to remember that they have been built for the honour and glory of God where the Creator, Redeemer and Sanctifier of mankind may be worshipped by his people. That is their first and primary function above all else. Nevertheless their importance as architectural, archaeological and historical monuments is profound.

To the Nation each parish church be it small and humble, or large and stately, is a record of history for herein lies the story of the parish: The wealth and prosperity of a community at any particular time is clearly reflected in the architectural form and decoration of the parish church. The history of the principal families is seen in the magnificent tombs and monuments. Changes in the pattern of liturgical worship is shown in much of its furnishings and alterations to furnishings. In fact there is no better way of learning about the history of the local community than by making a study of the parish church, for it was always so closely bound up with the life of the community and it was the centre of the social life of the parish.

The English parish churches are all so different in scale and in dimensions. In the first place we have the small Saxon churches consisting of two units—the altar house or chancel and the unit for the community known as the nave.

At the other end of the scale, we have the large churches with aisles, transepts and chapels, principally of 15th century date which can be seen to a great extent in East Anglia. In any appreciation of our ancient churches it is necessary to study how they were planned, and then to understand their use throughout history.

Origins of church planning

In Essex alone the story of church planning and the story of the way in which these churches have been used down the centuries to the present day is very clearly told.

First of all, we need to remind ourselves that the plan of a church building in this country has two distinct origins. From the north comes the simple arrangement brought by the Celtic missioners, while from the south a more sophisticated plan was introduced by St Augustine's mission from Rome. In the first instance the priest missioner built a small rectangular hut, most likely of timber, in which he placed his altar and kept his books and vessels. It had a doorway on one side above which he most likely placed the Christian symbol of the cross. The people of that area then built for themselves a larger hut of timber against the priest's small hut in order that they too might be protected from the elements. This resulted in a two-cell unit, a nave for the people and a chancel for the priest. The doorway in the priest's part developed later into the chancel arch and the symbol of the cross above this doorway into the Rood. This is best seen in such Essex churches as *Strethall* and *Chickney*. As to the materials employed for such a building, there is only one example in the use of timber remaining, and that is in the nave of *Greensted* church, near Ongar.

The typical church plan which came from the south by the missioners from Europe was known as the basilican plan. This type of building had a lofty hall along the sides of which were columns separating the hall from lateral aisles. At the far end the building terminated in a semi-circular apse on the chord of which stood the altar, and from this space there projected a low screen wall forming an enclosure known as the

19a. *Greensted-juxta-Ongar.*
Saxon timbers.

19b. *Corringham. Norman tower.*

19c. *Great Bentley.*
Norman south doorway.

19d. *Pentlow.*
Norman apse and chancel.

cancelli from which our word chancel is derived. When this type of building first came to England it consisted only of the Hall or nave and the apsidal chancel. Thus we still have a two-cell plan, but whereas the northern influence brought the square east ended chancel that from the south brought the apsidal termination. There stands at *Bradwell-on-Sea* in Essex the remains of a church built by the order of St Cedd, the first known missioner to Essex, who, incidentally, came from the north but used builders who came from overseas, for its plan is similar to other 7th century churches in South East England which all terminate with the Roman apse.

Norman churches

With the Norman invasion the apsidal termination became normal and such two-cell unit churches as at *Hadleigh* and *East Ham* in Essex are typical. Eventually the apse gave way to the Celtic square east end which was far simpler to build and to roof, and this termination remained constant throughout the mediaeval period. The Normans developed the aisle plan which was not favoured by the Saxons owing to difficulties in the construction of arcades. Perhaps the best example in Essex of an aisled church of this period is at *Castle Hedingham*.

In all churches orientation was essential. That is to say, the chancel had to be in the east and the nave west of it, and priest and worshippers faced towards the rising sun in accordance with tradition.

Towers

In the development of church planning the next important feature was the tower, unknown in this country until the 10th century. Although built for the purpose of housing bells to summon the faithful, they were also used for reasons of defence when the neighbourhood was threatened by hostile action. The principal position for this new feature was at the west end of the nave when the ground floor stage often acted as a porch, though there are plenty of examples where the tower was sited between nave and chancel which lead occasionally to a cruciform plan in which transepts were placed to the north and the south. At *Corringham* we have a good example of the tower sited at the west end of the nave while at *Boreham* can be seen the tower between nave and chancel.

This plan form of nave, chancel and tower remained unchanged until the end of the mediaeval period, though expansion took place by enlarging the areas of nave and chancel in an eastward and westward direction, and laterally by the building of aisles and chapels. The east end of an aisle invariably terminated with a chapel. In the case of a westward extension, this either took the form of extending the aisles to the north and south sides of the tower so that the west walls of the aisles and tower were in one straight line, or by taking down the tower, making the necessary extension and building a new tower at the west end of the extension.

Churches enlarged

As the result of liturgical development in the 13th century most churches were extended eastwards to allow more space for the rendering of the liturgy, and as the result of greater reverence being paid to the Mother of Our Saviour a Lady Chapel in her honour came to be built often alongside the chancel and separated from it by an arcade.

With a Lady Chapel added on one side of the chancel there invariably came to be built a chapel to balance it on the other side.

Towards the latter end of the mediaeval period a small sacristy was sometimes added on the north or south side of the chancel. Before that time vessels were kept in aumbry cupboards and books and vestments in chests, the priest always vesting at the altar.

Porches. 21a. *Downham, timbered, c. 1450.*

21b. *Little Oakley,*
through a buttress. c. 1330.

21c. *Newport,*
two-storied c. 1480.

Porches then came to be built either on the north or south sides of the nave according to the approach from the village, and later a further porch was added opposite to the main entrance porch for processional purposes. Some of these porches are of timber construction as at *South Benfleet,* while others are of stone with a room above known as a parvise as at *Thaxted.*

Although in its basic form the plan of a church consisted of two cells—an altar house and a room for lay worshippers—the ultimate size of the building at the close of the mediaeval period must not be measured by the size of the community which the church then served. The floor area of the building and indeed its architectural magnificence were entirely dependant upon the piety of the wealth and the munificence of the traders. Where trade flourished producing wealth the church buildings were enlarged as an advertisement of that industry and wealth, irrespective of the size of the population. In north Essex, Suffolk and Norfolk where the wool industry flourished there arose a "nouveau riche" class which advertised their wealth in the adornment of the parish church. It needs to be stressed that a church was enlarged or even rebuilt to the honour and glory of God but its increased area depended upon the money available, and not upon the need to seat a population of a certain number as though the sitting position was the principal liturgical posture for worshipping the Almighty. When many of our churches were built there were no seats since people stood for worship while the infirm went to the walls where stone benches can still be seen as at *All Saints, Maldon.*

Naves

The nave with no fixed seating was used as the Public Hall. It is important to remember that the church, being the focus of the social community, became the centre of all kinds of events which took place in the parish and there was no distinction between sacred and secular. All parish activities took place in the nave of the parish church, and these activities were consecrated by the Presence of God. Only the chancel of our churches was regarded as the Holy of Holies which, as a sacred place, was screened off by the chancel gates which were always kept locked out of service time. The great rood above the screen reminded those in the nave of the eternal Presence of God. As the chancel gates were locked so was the font with its cover securely locked to the stone bowl. The remains of the staple hooks, and in some cases the staple, can often still be seen. Thus it is that the church had uses other than the primary one of worship. There is evidence that the nave of the church was sometimes used as a market, but one of the important events which took place in the nave was the Church Ale Festival held at Christmas, Easter and Whitsun which was an occasion of feasting and dancing all of which took place in the church. The gaiety of these occasions is often shown in the carved corbellings which we sometimes see in church with men playing musical instruments.

In the 15th century, however, there began the building of the church house or hall which was then used for these Ale festivals and other parish functions with the result that the naves of our churches became solely used as a place for the parishioners to worship in, and wooden pew seating appeared with bench ends decorated with tracery or terminated with poppy heads.

Chancels

As to the chancel, we must not think when we see those choir stalls today that such form of seating existed in mediaeval times. The surpliced choir did not invade our churches until the 19th century. The only choir stalls within our chancels were those in the monastic or collegiate buildings and such old stalls with their misericords can still be seen in such buildings, but never in the ordinary parish church where the chancel was solely the area for the rendering of the Divine Liturgy.

22

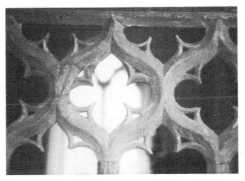

23b. *Bardfield Saling. Wooden rood screen c. 1350.*

23a. *Stebbing. Stone rood screen c. 1350.*

23c. *Writtle. Carpenter chantry.*

23d. *Bowers Gifford. Font c. 1500.*

Guilds and chantries

In mediaeval times the social life of the community was also bound up with numerous guilds and fraternities.

There were first of all the religious guilds, and then there were the guilds of merchants and craftsmen. The religious guilds were concerned with works of piety and charity, including the celebration of masses for souls of their departed brethren, while the other guilds were similar to the City Companies for the mutual benefit of the members. They played a very important part in the street processions, wearing their various liveries. They also were responsible for masses being said for the souls of their members.

In urban areas the guilds played a very important part, often exercising control in matters of local government. The great period of these guilds was after the Black Death in 1349 when it was necessary to conserve the interests of trade and craftsmanship.

As they flourished they often built for themselves a new porch to the church with a room above for the transaction of the business of the guild. They also added on to the church chapels which were guild chapels and they helped considerably in the general maintenance of the church buildings.

Each guild had its feast and they had a great love for pageants and mystery plays.

It has been stated that guilds and fraternities provided for masses being celebrated for the souls of their members, but masses were also said for departed souls by means of a chantry. What do we understand by chantry? It was a legal deed of obligation whereby a founder made arrangements for a mass to be celebrated at an altar in the church for the well-being of the benefactor during his lifetime, and for the granting of eternal rest for his soul after death.

The foundation of chantries became particularly popular in the 14th and 15th centuries and they brought the community into even closer association with their parish churches. The wealthy, the nobility, the lords of the manor and important ecclesiastics founded chantries for themselves and their families and most of these chantries were in connection with existing altars in the churches, although the more wealthy built their own chantry chapels, either within the church building or as an addition to the building by way of aisles and transepts. Some even built chantry chapels which were separate from the Parish Church. These chantries, however, were beyond the financial means of the ordinary humble layman, and in order not to be denied the benefit of masses for his soul, the people banded themselves together into a guild which was established for the mutual benefit of the members. So even the humble had the benefit of chantries and such chantries were usually associated with existing altars.

This meant an increase in clergy since every chantry had its own chantry priest, and a parish church might have had as many as five priests attached to it in addition to the parish priest. Where there were large numbers of chantry priests then the Diocesan Bishop would often lay down a rule for these priests to live communally within their own building under a rule, and the church very often became what is known as collegiate, with stalls for the priests forming a college, within the chancel of the church.

The church in the fifteenth century

In order to appreciate the appearance of our churches throughout the ages and the manner in which they were used, particularly subsequent to the mediaeval period, let us assume the possibility of a journey in time, and first of all visit the typical parish church in the 15th century. As we alight from our "time machine" and approach the church, we should at first notice that there were no tomb stones in the churchyard, the dead being commemorated in the prayers of the faithful and in the requiems celebrated by the parish priest or chantry priest. Nevertheless there would be a churchyard cross around which business would be often conducted. As we entered the church our nose would be drawn to the smell of sweet scented herbs, and we

25. Thaxted. Nave and aisle from the chancel.

should see the yew boughs and the herbs lying on the floor which when crushed by the feet, would give a pleasant aroma to counteract the smell of those who washed but little and seldom changed their clothes. There would be only one Mass on a Sunday and the whole parish would be assembled there, for everyone went to church. There might be a few pews since seating was beginning to find its way into the building, but only a few. A new piece of furniture would be the pulpit which began to appear towards the end of the 14th century, but it was a small feature shaped like a wineglass on a central stem. Above the chancel screen we should see the great rood, and above that, painted on the wall above the chancel arch would be a painting of the last judgement with the saved on one side, and the damned on the other being pitchforked by little black devils into the jaws of hell. Paintings would be seen on all walls, not for decorative purposes but as visual aids for the illiterate. They were in fact the poor Man's Bible. Here we should be able to see the miracles and parables of Our Lord as well as the story of the lives of the Saints. The church everywhere would be a riot of colour and especially the roofs. At the east end of each aisle we should see an altar screened off to form either a chantry chapel or a guild chapel where a separate priest was paid to say Masses for the departed. The chancel was the entire sanctuary. There would be no communion rails for communion was administered in the nave by the priest coming out through the screen for that purpose. We should see many shrines and lamps, the most important being the shrine of Our Lady, for England in mediaeval times was always known as Our Lady's Dowry.

The same church in the eighteenth century

Now let us travel in time to that same church in the 18th century. In the churchyard we should see a few monuments of local stone marking the graves of the well-to-do and the rising middle class. As we opened the church door we would be amazed to find a forest of pews—box pews lined with coloured baize with a high door into them from which, when seated, one could see nothing but the upper part of the arches of the arcade and the incumbent in his lofty stall and even loftier pulpit. This was the time of the three-decker, in the lowest sat the parish clerk, in the middle part facing the people was the incumbent, while from above he preached in a black gown for at least a whole hour. At the east end of the nave, and sometimes in the chancel, would be the elaborately decorated Squire's pew with perhaps a fireplace in it and if the sermon was too long he might get up and noisily stoke the fire. The walls were lime-washed and in certain places there were painted texts while over the chancel arch would be seen the Royal Arms. At the back of the church would be a gallery in which might be a barrel organ, though generally the music would be provided by viols and flutes. Beneath would be the hard seats for the charity children who would occasionally have to be admonished by the staff of the Parish Beadle. The servants might sit in side galleries, or on little ledges outside the pews of their masters. The communion table would be small. It would be fully covered by a red velvet cloth and it would be penned in by rails to keep the dogs from entering. Behind the communion table in framed boards would be painted the Lord's Prayer, the Creed and the Ten Commandments. On Communion Sunday at the words "Ye that do truly and earnestly repent", the faithful would leave their pews and follow the incumbent into the chancel and kneel around the altar for the rest of the service.

In *Messing* church can be seen today in the chancel what look like choir stalls. They are not, they are communion stalls. Here would sit those who "draw near with faith" into the chancel for the service of Holy Communion. The church would have a light appearance with clear glass windows, limewashed walls, and a ceiling inserted beneath the old timbered roof to make the church less cold.

The Victorian Era

Let us now move on a hundred years to the Victorian Era when the gentry and their tenants went to church in the morning and sent their servants to church in the

26

evening. A very different scene would confront us, as different from the 18th century as the 18th century was from mediaeval times.

In the churchyard the 18th century gravestones would be beginning to lean this way and that way, but the new feature would be the monuments in gleaming white marble taken from a monumental mason's catalogue with sentimental inscriptions in a crude form of lettering which usually strike a harsh note in so peaceful a setting.

When we enter the church we find that the box pews have gone and they have been replaced by a suitable type of pitch pine gothic pew wherever it is possible to place one. The general smell of the church would be of oil lamps, or gas lamps if the church is in a town, combined with the odour of furniture polish. The windows would now be filled with stained glass in which olive green would perhaps be the predominant colour. A new chancel screen might perhaps have been erected and on one side we should see a large pulpit, perhaps in alabaster balanced on the other side by a highly polished brass eagle. The chancel would appear cluttered with choir stalls and clergy stalls and would no longer be the sanctuary of mediaeval times. That part of the chancel referred to as the sanctuary would be a small area at the east end separated by rails of glittering brass. The altar most likely would be raised on a large number of steps to a level far above that in mediaeval times, making nonsense of the sedilia and piscina on the south side of the chancel which would be at almost ground level. There would be little colour since colour would have been regarded as ritualistic. The floors would be paved with black and red tiles and on the walls we should see brass tablets to the memory of worthy churchwardens now long forgotten.

The church today

Let us now see the same church today and what would we find? Internally as well as externally we would notice a marked improvement in the standard of maintenance and repair, due largely to the Inspection of Churches Measure whereby all churches are now compulsorily inspected by an architect every five years. The church is now kept clean and tidy and the walls would probably have been recently limewashed. Unnecessary pews have been removed creating some open spaces especially at the back of the church where coffee is now served after Sunday service. In fact the nave has returned to the use it had in mediaeval times for all parish activities as well as for normal worship. We should probably find that the chancel has become much changed. Enthusiasm for singing has led to large choirs with additional benches placed in front of the 19th century ones, in consequence of which only the narrowest of passageways exists in the approach to the altar, which itself has been brought forward to allow the celebrant to take the westward position. In some cases we might find that the mediaeval chancel has almost become abandoned and a new sanctuary has been created at the eastern end of the nave with some of the pews removed so that the congregation sit further westwards. We might even find that the axis of the church has been turned round 90 degrees. Whatever may have been gained in clarity in the new ways of worship current today, there is so often a loss in mystery and in the sense of the numinous so vital to all our worship.

In spite of all contemporary fashion, and indeed gimmicks, which can only be of a temporary nature, the old mediaeval church still stands much loved and cherished, a building of infinite appeal to all sorts and conditions of men.

Whether the church is seen in the golden light of a summer's evening or snow laden against a leaden sky it remains to tell the story of the religious, the cultural and the economic history of the parish and long may that continue. The rich collection of mediaeval parish churches which we have received from our forebears must be cherished and preserved no matter what the cost may be for we are only its temporary trustees. Thus, and thus only, will our descendants be able to appreciate and enjoy this glorious national heritage of English mediaeval church architecture.

THE CHURCH IN ELIZABETHAN ESSEX

F.G. Emmison

As is well known, many churches suffered disastrously through the changes which the Reformation enforced. No longer were the people to see religious 'images' lest they attracted worship for 'superstitious uses'. So, in Henry VIII's last year and Edward VI's first years ecclesiastical instructions led to the wanton destruction or defacement of countless statues and crosses. Down came not only the great rood (cross) but also the rood-screen with its woodcarvings. Wall-paintings were covered by whitewash, but the taking down of stained glass windows resulted in their inevitable destruction. Bells and altars were removed, the latter being replaced by the simple 'Lord's table'. Missals and other church books, often illuminated, were destroyed on account of their alleged dedication to superstition. The rich vestments were discarded in favour of plain ones. The intensity of the religious zeal was extended to church plate, which gave way to simple 'communion cups'. One by one, the artistic glories of the medieval churches went in this violent anti-Rome wave.

The short-lived return to the Old Faith under Mary could do nothing to reverse the great physical losses. The hasty swings of the politico-religious pendulum led the great mass of the ordinary people to welcome the compromise effected by the Church Settlement of 1559. But not all had gone in the pre-1553 iconoclastic surge. Some of the Elizabethan bishops therefore decreed more complete compliance with Reformation tenets.

Edmund Grindal, the first Elizabethan Bishop of London, exhorted the clergy and churchwardens in his diocese (which then included the whole of Essex) to demolish the high stone altars and to provide communion tables in their place. Shrines and images, mural paintings or other pictures that had survived the Edwardian destruction were now to be removed as idolatrous; but stained glass still *in situ* was accorded some respite.

William Harrison, the vicar of *Radwinter*, in his famous *Description of England* (1577), faithfully chronicled the stipulated changes in a concise passage, with a valuable reference to stained glass:

All images, shrines, tabernacles, rood-lofts and monuments of idolatry are removed, taken down and defaced; only the stories in glass windows excepted, which, for want of sufficient store of new stuff, and by reason of extreme charge that should grow by the alteration of the same into white panes through the realm are not altogether abolished in most places at once, but by little and little suffered to decay, that white glass may be provided and set up in their rooms. Finally, whereas there was wont to be a great partition between the choir and the body of the church, now it is either very small or none at all.

It is to the credit of the Elizabethan clergy and wardens that the stained glass was not smashed in some churches. Iconoclasm had gone far enough, many thought, whether tolerant or just practical-minded (but much of what was then left was swept away by the Commonwealth wave). Fortunately, a few white-washed mural paintings have now been uncovered and restored, as at *Great Canfield, Little Easton, Hadleigh, Fairstead* and *Little Baddow*; and we still can admire the renowned work at *Copford* church.

Preserved among the records of the Archdeaconry of Essex (which covered the southern half of the county) is a register of the Archdeacon's important Visitation of 1565, into which were copied the returns made by the churchwardens for 139 of the 145 parishes under his jurisdiction.

Delays in removing the rood loft were referred to in several parishes, e.g. 'Certain boards over the rood loft remain unpulled down' (*Bulphan*) and 'The rood loft is pulled down one part of it, and the rest is left for fear of the church falling' (*West*

29a. Elizabethan Pulpits. *Clavering.*

29b. *Bardfield Saling.*

29c. Elizabethan church chairs. *Stambourne.*

29d. *East Mersea.*

29

Horndon: the church vanished long ago). At *Vange*, ' The choir is unpaved and the place where the altar stood not whited, but is as it was when the altar was plucked down, and it is all unglazed'. A unique entry is made under *St Peter, Maldon:* 'There is an altar standing still in the spittle (hospital), to the offence of the people' (the slight remains of the leper hospital still stands by the side of the Chelmsford road). 'The imagery in the glass windows are not all defaced' was the position in *Stanford Rivers;* and 'There is a beam whereon was wont to stand a light before an image called Our Lady, which Mr Tyrrell will not suffer to be pulled down' at *Little Warley;* these are solitary items. Perhaps John Tyrrell, the Catholic lord of the manor, still hoped that the religious tide would turn once again and he would then be able to replace the light. The renowned Saxon church of *Greensted-by-Ongar* was the only one the wardens of which confessed to having no communion cup (its present cup is dated 1739).

Disobedience regarding vestments was reported only from *South Ockendon,* where 'there be certain vestments and other church goods used in the time of popery undefaced'. What is probably the last list of pre-Reformation Essex church vestments is recorded for *South Weald*: ' There were sold by the bishop's warrant one cope of white damask, two vestments of blue velvet, one old cope of blue damask, one vestment and a cope of bridges (Bruges) satin, two old tunicles of Turkey silk, two old vestments of fustian, and one altar cloth of imagery work'; these were sold to four named men.

Fairly typical of the whole country is the chronicle for Essex of the almost wholesale loss of mediaeval church plate at the dissolution of the religious houses, guilds and chantries under Henry VIII and Edward VI; followed by purchase of new plate under Mary; then its sale or adaptation, or more generally the obligatory purchase in Elizabeth's early years of a 'fair and comely cup' called a communion cup, in place of the 'massing chalice'. This is what the churchwardens' accounts of *Great Dunmow* say about the change-over. In 1558 they sold two chalices weighing 23¼ oz. for £6 15s.5d., buying in their place 'the communion cup weighing 17 oz., £6 7s.' Next year the 'chief inhabitants' agreed that the wardens should sell crosses and the like, weighing a total of 110 oz. worth 5s. 4d. the oz., i.e. £29 6s.8d. But a few pieces of pre-Reformation plate fortunately escaped destruction, and these are described, with photographs, in *Church Plate of Essex,* 1926. And many Essex churches still possess the early Elizabethan plate; 'very fine examples of their period, being not only graceful in design, but having elaborate and well-executed decorative features, exhibiting a great variety of detail.'

In the years following the Visitation of 1565 the archives of the Archdeacons of Essex and Colchester provide a sad indictment of the neglect of the fabric of many Essex churches and chancels: the former were, of course, the responsibility of the parishioners through the churchwardens, the latter that of the rector (or in the case of a vicar that of the lay rector). Although it is a well-accepted fact that numerous churches were in a structurally bad state at the beginning of the reign, most of the reports or charges fall within the last fifteen years. The Archdeacon's court usually instructed the wardens to effect the necessary repairs within a few months and to certify their having done so.

'Gingmountney' (*Mountnessing*) wardens presented, 'The church is ruined, viz. the steeple' (1566). In the same year *Loughton* 'steeple' was so 'ruinous' that the bells could not be rung (steeple means the tower). '*Asheldham* steeple lieth half unshingled' (1576), and again, 'The steeple is in great decay' (1578). The entry accusing the *Woodford* wardens of neglect has a note, 'The church is like to fall down' (1579). *St Martin's* church at *Colchester* was perhaps in a worse condition: 'Our church with all things belonging are very unrepaired and ready to fall down' (1587). The efforts of later wardens evidently failed to restore it, and another charge was made, to which the answer was, 'Our church is greatly in decay and we are not able to make it' (1591). That is 'probably fell down in the seventeenth century' was the opinion of the inspector of the Royal Commission on Historical Monuments in 1922. Four centuries before their church was to be totally destroyed by fire (1971), the

Alresford wardens also pleaded poverty: 'The steeple is ruinous and our church not so well tiled as it ought to be, but our parish is very poor and we cannot invoke them to make a new rate for the reparation' (1587). A few weeks afterwards the court learned that *Lawford* church was 'greatly decayed and the steeple is fallen down'. And a similar sad story emerges regarding other Essex churches.

We may now describe a few facets of 'church life' in Elizabethan Essex, of which little was known before recent studies of the archidiaconal records. Perhaps the most remarkable discovery is the extraordinary number and variety of disturbances and quarrels which took place, especially during or immediately after divine service. Month after month the courts dealt with cases of layman insulting or assaulting layman or churchwarden; layman disturbing, mocking, slandering, or even striking cleric; occasionally, too, cleric abusing or attacking layman; or, twice, cleric quarrelling with cleric. Many of these squabbles arose, of course, from the large and partly irreligious congregations present owing to compulsory attendance. On the other hand, a few of the troubles arose from differences of opinion in an age when liturgical aspects of the services were vital questions with some of the earnest laymen.

The disorders usually arose out of rude remarks, e.g. in 1596 William Chesshier presented for 'swearing, banning (cursing) and railing' in *Wix* church, 'calling Thomas Stowe rascally knave, tinkerly knave, the boy'. Perhaps the most intriguing incident was that which caused the wardens of *Great Tey* in 1600 to present Henry Hazellwood of *Coggeshall*. 'He and divers companions misdemeaned themselves in our church in sermon and service time that day that one of them was killed'. The accused's statement ran, 'He went and sat among the maids, and he did go up a ladder as to make a sermon'. The irreverence of many was of a more passive nature. Some dozed off quietly and briefly unobserved, but the stentorian slumberers who 'sleep offensively' could not be ignored, nor could those who 'continually sleep in time of divine service'. Four men slept in *Heydon* church in 1597, but the record for somnolence goes to *Ramsey*. Was it a very sultry Sunday or a very long sermon? At any rate, in July of the same year 'There were 18 that slept in the church, and some of them being told thereof by the churchwardens did defy them and bade them to do what they could'.

Many a fracas occurred when the congregation made their exit into the churchyard. 'Railing' or 'buffeting each other' there was a very common delinquency. Brabbling in the churchyard and calling another 'dolt, ass, fool and knave' was admitted by a *Weeley* man. In *Earls Colne* churchyard John Reynolds, a butcher, struck Thomas Allen and drew blood in 1582. Bloodshed was only just avoided at *Colne Engaine* in 1595 when Amos Manship 'brabbled and quarrelled at the church door in sermon time with three men, and in the quarrel his wife did draw her knife in the churchyard, as she hath confessed'. But the court records of course are silent about the large number of devout parishioners, and we know from other documents that some travelled several miles to other churches because 'godly and long sermons' were not accorded them in their own parishes.

The building of new churches in Elizabethan England was a rare event. In Essex, *Woodham Walter* is the sole example; this mellow red-brick building was consecrated by the Archdeacon of Essex in 1564. The period was remarkably barren in providing new furnishings, as fonts and pews. The big exception, of course, is communion plate. But why, in an age in which supreme importance was attached by many to the sermon, and especially in puritan Essex, have we virtually no surviving Elizabethan pulpits except those at *Clavering* and *Bardfield Saling* ?

Television usually portrays the Elizabethan Age by way of the Queen's ultra-colourful Court, omitting to state that it represented less than one-thousandth of the population. For the great mass of the people, life was rude and living often little above subsistence level. It is against such a background that my study of the Essex Church records has convinced me that most of the 800 churchwardens elected annually carried out their duties with such care and commonsense as was expected of the farmer and tradesmen classes who bore the main responsibilities.

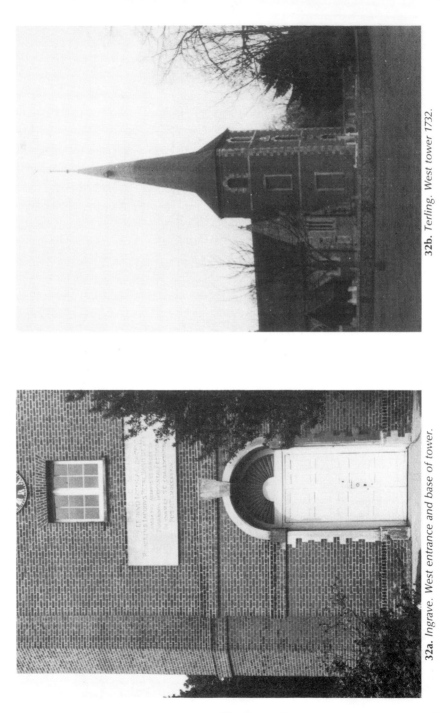

32b. Terling. West tower 1732.

32a. Ingrave. West entrance and base of tower.

THE EIGHTEENTH CENTURY

D.F. Stenning

Essex is not well endowed with churches of the eighteenth century. The most notable complete church is that at *Wanstead* (1787/90) by Thomas Hardwick, a grand neo-classical building, with a fine interior. *St Peter and St Paul, Shellow Bowells*, 1754, is now a house and is a simple unassuming brick structure, with an archaic hybrid roof structure. The other partial 18th Century constructions are noticeably individual; mediaeval reminiscences, vernacular quaintness and touches of the old-fashioned baroque, provide a certain piquancy.

St Nicholas', Ingrave is generally considered to have been entirely rebuilt in 1735, and stands within a pentangular churchyard with dilapidated, but contemporary, iron railings. The west tower is a singular conception, square in plain, with octagonal turrets on the north and south faces, rising above the main parapet. The unusual design, seemingly influenced by work of Vanbrugh or Hawksmoor seems a separate build earlier than the main body of the church behind. At the base there is a very grand entrance with a pair of doors, under a semi-circular stone dressed arch. The central two-thirds is relieved only by an arch headed belfry opening and an inscribed plaque, the large expanse of good red brickwork (with bad modern pointing) in sharp contrast with the decorative arcaded corbel tables near the parapet.

The nave and narrower chancel to the east have more of a non-conformist character; simple bold string course and regularly spaced, arch headed and oval windows, a heavy timber cornice and fine pegtiled roof. The nave has central paired doors on its long sides, produces a cross axis, as at the Adam church of *Mistley*. The interior is of plain plasterwork, with a semi-circular chancel arch on very overscaled inpost mouldings.

A touch more sophisticated is the west tower of *All Saints, Terling*. An inscribed tablet on the west wall provides the date 1732, and the mason, Antony Goud, who is known to have worked with Leoni at Moulsham Hall. It is broad and solid, divided conventionally into three stages, with a tall plinth, the proportions a little unconvincing. The north and south walls are of Flemish bond, with a diaper of black headers and red stretchers, the west, all of red brick and the east seems part of an earlier build. The detail has a Palladian basis, portland stone quoins on all stages (a visual substitute for mediaeval buttresses), narrow stone string bands and arched openings to the belfry, the west door and to a window in the stage above it. All the arched openings have stone quoins and triple keystones and the north and south walls have square headed blank recesses in the lower two stages with plain stone surrounds. The Palladian character is undermined by the homely diapering of the north and south walls and the crowding of motifs in the west wall, which produces a strong vertical emphasis. The composition is completed by a "cornice" of brick string bands from the contemporary domestic vernacular and surmounted, rather unexpectedly, by a tall shingled broach spire of excellent proportions. There is also a small 18th century English bond and diapered vestry, with fine rubbed brick pointed arches, diagonal buttresses, with a gable pediment with trefoil oculus all with thin stone detail.

The greatest curiosity is the little twelfth century church at *Lambourne* which was extensively remodelled in 1742. The west entrance beneath the miniature-brooch spire has a wide flat canopy on carved acanthus brackets and a pair of raised and fielded panel doors all of a distinctly domestic character. Within, the massive late-medieval belfry frame is largely obscured by a west gallery of 1704, suitably inscribed, as the gift of William Walter, a London ironmonger. This has small panels of carved ornament and is supported on four substantial posts, the upper part of each takes the form of stumpy doric columns.

In 1742 new windows were provided, broad but slightly pointed in the nave and

34a. *Ingrave. Tower and stair turret.*

34b. *Harlow. Potter Street Baptist Chapel.*

with semi-circular arches in the chancel. A low chancel arch was formed of eliptical profile and springing from muscular paired console brackets, the composition strangely reminiscent of renaissance bridge design. The arch soffit has four bold coffer-like panels with quatre foils inset, the detail generally being amusingly overscaled.

The fifteenth century roof structure posed an unprecedented problem. Our unknown designer, encased the tie beams in plaster with an emphatic key pattern on the soffits. The quadrant braces of the crown post he clothed with acanthus and the post became a Serlioesque, square column. In all, a remarkably inventive solution even excepting the "swollen cabbage" like form of the acanthus.

The chancel received a plaster vault with bosses and an interlace of cable mouldings suggestive of quadripartite subdivisions. Cornices of somewhat coarse profile surround nave and chancel, with similar mouldings framing the openings, taking the form of an ogee with crest, over the east window. Altogether this remarkable facelift of 1742 produced a unified interior although mixing "Gothick" and mildly baroque detail in a touchingly unscholarly manner.

In its massiveness the west tower of *St Peter's, Colchester*, has a positive Roman quality. Built in 1758 and forming an exciting element of the townscape of North Hill, it compares very satisfactorily with the perpendicular work. Inside, the lower stages are circular, like the interior of a windmill. Large circular openings on the north and south faces of the clock stage reveal the enormous thickness of brickwork. The detail otherwise is a little tame with quoins and ineffectual battlements, of gault stocks contrasting with dull red bricks in English and Flemish bond. The western doorcase with its fanlight introduces a "Gothick" note and the interior has sensible eighteenth century galleries.

The best known eighteenth century Essex church, is that at *Mistley*. Built circa 1735 as a simple rectangular box, it was extended in 1776 to the design of Robert Adam. This created a building of great originality, with tuscan porticos on the shorter axis and identical towers at the east and west. The twin towers now well tended by the Department of the Environment are of three major stages. The base with free standing tuscan columns, a central square attic, with pediments on each face and a tall circular ionic collonaded lantern with leaded dome. Although sophisticated in the usual Adam neo-classical manner, the open free standing columns of the base and the atenuated profile of the lanterns, are faintly suggestive of eighteenth century "Gothick". The east tower contains some of its original decoration and the west a semi-circular window, with delicate fan pattern of iron glazing bars.

The church of *St Mary and All Saints, Debden* is of singular curiosity and charm. In 1786, the medieval nave and aisles were extensively repaired gaining battlemented parapets, numerous pinnacles and a refaced west end. The stonework detail is neat and delicate, "Gothick" detail with classical clarity and even a thinly disguised pediment over the west window. In the same year, a new font was provided, designed by Richard Holland, architect and builder, brother of the celebrated Henry Holland. This is of Coade stone, noticeably more correct in its medieval detail and intricately modelled in this hard smooth material. The mysterious architect, James Essex, erected a new steeple in 1786 and although, now rebuilt, a plaque in the vestry commemorates the event—"Ingenious Mr. Essex, Architect, late of Cambridge, Deceased."

A further campaign of works was carried out in 1792, this time designed by John Carter, antiquarian and former draughtsman to Henry Holland. This, built by Richard Holland, is the most intriguing part of the eighteenth century work, and consists of an octagonal sanctuary, or chapel, linked to the nave by a lower short chancel. Externally the detail is hand and mechanical, faced in the Hollands favourite Suffolk white brick and with medallions of Coade stone in alternate bays. Comparison of the pinnacles, with those of the earlier stage, emphasises an increasingly archaeological attitude to the "Gothick" style.

Within, the effect is remarkable. The octagon, based on York Minster chapter house, has a ribbed vaulted plaster ceiling and was originally screened from the chancel by a pair of extra oak columns. The "chancel" has peculiar spikey pendant arcading and provides a necessary visual transition between octagon and nave.

Viewed from the lower floor level of the nave, the effect is quite theatrical. Black timber ribs and cusps reminiscent of bats wings, and two elegant oval wall monuments (by King of Bath) convey a strange boudoir flavour. "A pleasing and awful sensation" is how a collaborator of John Carter had described a previous chapel commission; it seems equally appropriate here. Also worthy of attention are a boldly carved and painted Royal Arms in surround and the delicate and elaborate tomb-chest of the patron Richard Chiswell.

There are also a number of attractive non-conformist chapels. That at *Terling* has very early eighteenth century qualities, a hipped pegtile roof, patterned brickwork and mullioned and transomed windows. That at *Harlow* (1756) has an exuberant doorcase in its gabled front elevation.

THE GOTHIC REVIVAL

Peter C.E. Elers

Introduction

The ecclesiastical and architectural heritage of Essex is rich and varied and by no means confined to our many ancient churches. Indeed, we need to be careful that we do not evaluate a church building merely according to its age but rather for the quality of its design and craftsmanship regardless of when it was built. At least a hundred of the 19th and early 20th century church buildings in Essex are of considerable importance, some are of outstanding beauty and interest. But all too often they go unnoticed and remain unappreciated, they are costly to heat and maintain, they may no longer be in the centre of the parish. They are, therefore, ideal candidates for redundancy, ripe for pastoral reorganization and valuable money raisers as potential supermarket sites. A number have already gone that way. Go and have a look at the churches mentioned in this essay: it may help you to view your own church with fresh appreciation and enjoyment and make you more anxious to preserve it for posterity from the developer.

The Gothic shape

A feeling for the Gothic shape, i.e. the pointed arch, began to creep back during the 18th century: it provided a pleasant contrast to the rather severe formal lines of the current Classical style. The earliest example of Gothic Revival I have found in Essex is at *Debden* near Saffron Walden where in 1793 John Carter added to the medieval church an octagonal chancel in white brick decorated with pinnacles without and a ribbed plaster vault complete with pendants within—a charming and highly original design. The rebuilding of *Harwich* by M.G. Thompson followed in 1821, the nave still with galleries on three sides but with a groined vault, the chancel a shallow apse, the windows neo-Perpendicular.

For a short time the pendulum swung right back to the pre-Gothic Romanesque architecture. *Colchester St Botolph* by W. Mason of Ipswich in 1837 took its cue from the Norman Priory ruins alongside: it is big and bold, all its arches are semicircular, yet the interior retains galleries under a single roof concealed inside by tunnel and groined vaults. Adie Repton's *Springfield Holy Trinity* (1843) is similar in style on a smaller scale. The most successful neo-Norman design is *Loughton St John Baptist* by Sydney Smirke (1846), a cruciform building without aisles or galleries and with a flat-topped central square tower. Incidentally this church is greatly enhanced by its Baroque furnishings combining marble and mosaic with Pre-Raphaelite stained glass. But on the whole the pointed arch prevailed. So Edward Blore built lancet-style parish churches for *Leytonstone* and *Stratford* in 1832, each in yellow brick with an asymmetrically placed tower. James Savage was more conventional in giving his galleried *Ilford St Mary* a west tower (and formerly spire). *Rivenhall* is a fascinating rebuild of 1838, its slender tower having enormous turrets, its Y-shaped windows a wealth of medieval stained glass brought back from the Continent by a former rector. Most surprising of all is Mason's *East Donyland* (1838), a stock brick replica of an octagonal Early English chapter house with groups of five stepped lancets and a steeply pointed roof. Lewis Vulliamy introduced panels of flushwork flint in the East Anglian tradition in the nave walls of *Chingford St Peter and St Paul* in 1844.

Thinking in Gothic

By the middle of the 19th century architects were beginning to think in Gothic as opposed to applying Gothic motifs to auditorium-type buildings. Chancels and sanctuaries begin to assume greater importance, and aisles and arcades abound. As

Pugin had opened people's eyes to English Gothic as true 'Christian architecture', so Ruskin and the increased facilities for continental travel brought back a further interpretation of Gothic from France and Italy. It influenced James Brooks whose impressive *Plaistow St Andrew* (1870) towers over its surroundings, neo-Early English in detail yet with a tall clerestory, chancel screen and unfinished crossing tower, while his humbler *Southend-on-Sea All Saints* (1889) in dark red brick has tiers of equal lancets at the east end. William Burges' reconstruction of the east wall of *Waltham Abbey* (1859) similarly reflects French influence with its forceful wheel window and massive carved stonework, reminiscent of the impressive stiff-leaf capitals and wheel window at *Chigwell Row* by Seddon (1867). E.C. Lee's only two surviving churches are both in Essex and worth a visit: *Brentwood St Thomas* has a splendid north-west tower and soaring spire with spirelets and a seemingly endless clerestory of lancets leading to a Sanctus bellcote, *Bentley Common* is on smaller scale but beautifully proportioned, also with grouped lancets. Dollman's freestanding tower and broach spire at *Walthamstow St Saviour* dominate the Lea Valley, though the church is not as grand as it was having lost its pitched roof in a fire. When S.S. Teulon built in yellow, red and black brick and gave his spires little or no tower, as at *Silvertown St Mark* (1861), his designs strike our modern eyes as grotesquely ugly. Yet he reconstructed *South Weald* accurately and pleasantly in 1868 and designed the charmingly situated church at *Birch* with an asymmetrical broach spire and Decorated tracery in 1850. Lastly in this group Giles and Gane's high French Gothic *Victoria Docks St Luke* (1874) deserves a mention.

Prolific architects

The really prolific church architects of the period have all contributed works to Essex. Sir George Gilbert Scott designed two excellent churches in the *Halstead* area, *Holy Trinity* (1843) in the Early English style with a free standing broach spire, *Greenstead Green* (1845) in neo-Decorated with a western octagonal tower and spire. His *Wanstead Christ Church* (1861) on the other hand is long and low with plate tracery. In addition he restored a number of Essex churches, as did William Butterfield who boldly added a lofty polychromatic tiled chancel to the Saxon nave at *Hadstock* and rebuilt *Ardleigh* in 1881 all but the tower and porch. Ewan Christian gave his new Early English church at *Wickham Bishops* (1850) a heavy broach spire with an overhang which makes it a landmark and neighbouring *Tiptree* (1855) sweeping roofs over nave and aisles and reticulated tracery. The Cutts brothers built numerous lofty brick churches in the London area, all with a bell turret, grouped lancet windows and pleasing stone arcades: those in the Chelmsford diocese include *Forest Gate St Edmund, Ilford St Alban* and *Victoria Docks The Ascension*. Hakewill's churches by contrast are all in grey stone and rural surroundings, at *Beaumont-cum-Moze* with an unusual Decorated bell turret, at *Aldham* and *Myland* with tall spires.

G.E. Street rebuilt *Hutton* accurately and carefully in 1873, while new churches were provided for *Twinstead* by Henry Woodyer (1860), with fanciful brick decoration in the style of his master Butterfield, and *Langdon Hills* by William White (1876), a very tall and narrow building dramatically perched on top of a ridge. Sir Reginald Blomfield must have rivalled Scott in his colossal output: *Colchester St John* (1862) is a typical early work in many ways more attractive than the much larger *St Mary-at-the Walls* (1872). *High Beech* (1873) is a pleasant stone Early English church deep in Epping Forest, *Forest Gate All Saints* and *Leytonstone St Andrew* large clerestoried buildings dominating their urban surroundings, the latter recently interestingly divided for contemporary use. Blomfield's eastern additions to *Chingford St Peter and St Paul* in the Perpendicular style (1903), a posthumous work, are cleverly linked with the Vulliamy nave by a triple arch. St Aubyn deserves a mention for his twin spires which flank Chelmsford on the south, *Widford* (1862) and *Galleywood* (1873).

36a. Theydon Bois. One of Sydney Smirke's least attractive designs in red brick (1850) in a beautiful forest setting.

36b. Wicken Bonhunt. A charming and idiosyncratic rebuild of 1858-9 designed by the Rector, the Revd John Hanson Sperling.

36c. Pleshey. The cruciform plan and central tower were dictated by the foundations of medieval church replaced by Chancellor in 1868.

Local architects

Sometimes incumbents have been sufficiently skilled to rebuild or decorate their churches. Such were the Rev. Charles Smith who rebuilt *Little Canfield* in 1839 with much ornate decoration, some weird window tracery, contemporary stained glass and a miniature spire, and the Rev. Ernest Geldart who added to and embellished the tiny Norman church at *Little Braxted* with a complete set of wall paintings and Tractarian furnishings. Local or diocesan architects have also left their mark: Chancellor rebuilt the cruciform church at *Pleshey* with a crossing tower in 1868 and a new church in brick at *Ford End* where four large Evangelists with haloes resembling soup-plates gaze down from the tower. Charles Spooner built large cool red brick churches with pantiled roofs and flèches at *Little Ilford St Michael* (1897) and *Aldersbrook* (1914), while Sir Charles Nicholson contributed no less than eight new churches. All but one are vaguely Perpendicular and they all have white walls and coloured roofs. The earliest, *Westcliff-on-Sea St Alban* (1898) has fine furnishings by him as well, while *St Michael* (1926) has an apse at both ends. *Frinton-on-Sea* and *Becontree St Elizabeth* are light and airy, while *Grays All Saints* and *Southchurch Christ Church* are more homely. *Barkingside St George* (1931) has a squat tower and exciting modern engraved glass. *Leigh-on-Sea St Margaret* is completely different: here Nicholson freely mixed Classical and Romanesque, culminating in a semicircular apse. Far less known and admired than he ought to be is Edwin Dunn whose four lovely churches in a modern version of the Perpendicular style are all in the *Ilford* area. He completed *St Mary's* with a magnificent chancel approached by a great flight of steps from the Savage nave, and designed three new churches using a rich red brick unashamedly for every detail including the tracery and mullions of the windows: the effect is most satisfying. *Ilford St Margaret* (1914), *St Luke* (1941) and *Woodford Green St Barnabas* are all well worth a visit.

Masterpieces

The most outstanding Gothic Revival churches in Essex are, however, in most cases single examples of an architect's work. James Fowler for instance did *South Woodford Holy Trinity* in a neo-Transitional style in 1887, Eden Nesfield rebuilt *Radwinter* with its sumptuous Tractarian interior and elaborate wrought iron work in 1869. Another Anglo Catholic shrine, vast and awe-inspiring, is *Walthamstow St Michael*, designed by a young man, James Maltby Bignell, in 1885, the year of his death: its scale is enormous, its details such as pillars and capitals unique. Sir Walter Tapper's masterpiece, *Southend-on-Sea St Erkenwald* (1905), towers like a cliff face over the surrounding boarding houses: its internal proportions and canted chancel are superb.

W. D. Caroe has two marvellous churches in Essex, *Stansted Mountfitchet St John* with a richly pinnacled tower like a crown and *Walthamstow St Barnabas* (1902) strongly influenced by Art Nouveau with a brick traceried triforium, splendid proportions, highly original window tracery with contemporary glass, but now under serious threat as the result of dry rot. Basil Champneys' little flint church at *Havering atte Bower* (1875) has a charming exterior with its freestanding tower, as on a much larger scale has *Epping*, one of the finest works of Bodley and Garner (begun in 1889) with its pinnacled tower (1909) and great east window dominating the High Street and inside a wealth of carved wood and gilding—a church not to be missed on any account. Nor is its neighbour, *Upshire* , by the Buxton Estate architects, Freeman and Ogilvy, in 1902, with its shingled spire, sweeping roofs and timber arcade (was it cut from the surrounding forest, I wonder?): be sure to notice the door hinges and latches, the king-post roof and the light fittings. Temple Moore gave *Radwinter* its flint tower in 1887 and designed *Clacton-on-Sea St James* in 1913. Don't be put off by the exterior: inside it is breathtaking with a great sweep of steps leading to the colourful high altar and simplified Perpendicular architecture which is deliberately

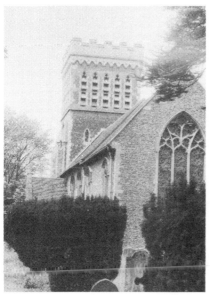

38a. *Foxearth. An original and powerful tower of 1862 which unfortunately lost its towering spire in 1947.*

38b. *Stanford-le-Hope. This bold and richly decorated replica of the 15th century tower at Prittlewell was added in 1883.*

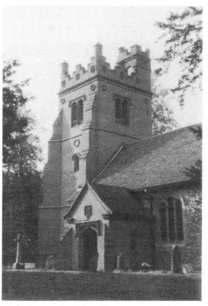

38c. *Cranham. A particularly pleasing and well placed broach spire relieved by single lucarnes (1874).*

38d. *Inworth. The diocesan architect, Joseph Clarke, added this massive red brick tower in 1876.*

asymmetrical throughout. Sir Ninian Comper and F. C. Eden made noble additions to *Southchurch Holy Trinity* in 1906 and 1932, and we have one church by Comper himself in his inimitable free Perpendicular style—*Manor Park St Barnabas*.

Another "one off" is *Ilford St Andrew*, a vast brick church in which Sir Herbert Baker employed an unusual fusion of Romanesque and Gothic shapes with pleasing result in 1924. No survey of Essex churches of this period could be complete without including the most perfect example of Art Noveau in the country, *Great Warley* by Harrison Townsend with metal font and screen by Reynolds-Stephens and glass by Heywood Sumner. Outside the church has overhanging eaves and is roughcast just like a Voysey house, inside the tunnel vault and the apse are decorated in silver. Finally, mention must be made of Harold Gibbons' rebuilding of *Plaistow St Philip and St James* after the war in a highly original free Gothic idiom, golden brick with a small campanile outside, all white within, a mixture of English and Italian motifs, contemporary yet timeless.

These are some of the more outstanding examples which the 19th and early 20th centuries have contributed to Essex church building. I recommend them as being well worth a visit and careful study, for many of them have as much to contribute to the greater glory of God and to our enjoyment as have the more famous buildings of earlier centuries.

CHURCH CARPENTRY

C.A. Hewett

The carpentry to be found in Essex churches provides a field for study to which little systematic attention has been paid in the past. Most examples can be placed in convenient categories, but there are two which defy classification.

The timber-built carcase of the church of *St Andrew* at *Greensted-juxta-Ongar* is Saxon work that owes its survival to the credibility of its association with St Edmund. The remains of St Edmund, King and Martyr, were translated c.1013 to Bedriceworth (subsequently Bury St. Edmund's) and were accommodated one night in a *lignea capella* at "Aungre", as Dugdale quoted in his *Monasticon* from a very early source in the Lambeth Library. There can be no serious doubt that the "wooden chapel" was Greensted, but examination of its fabric disposes of the legend that the church was built for the event, rather than utilised because existing and suitably situated on the route from London to Bury. Had it been built for the event it must, surely, have been dedicated to St Edmund rather than to St Andrew. Contemporary evidence for such churches is provided by the Venerable Bede, writing during the seventh century, with specific reference to Bishop Aidan's episcopal church in the Isle of Lindisfarne; this was *non de lapide, sed de robore secto totam composuit*. This provides grounds for ascribing Greensted church to some time between the end of the seventh and the opening of the tenth centuries. A limited and recent excavation has proved that the site supported an earlier wooden church with earthfast posts, but the date of the existing structure remains uncertain. It is possible for similar log-walls to have survived elsewhere disguised as rubble or masonry walls—as the other rarity suggests.

This is the south aisle of the church of *St Thomas the Apostle* at *Navestock,* which is built of timber and was always disguised as masonry. The arcade comprises five double-chambered arches, framed in timber, supported by four oaken piers and two terminal responds. The timber was heavily plastered and the piers finished as circular, with appropriate capitals and bases of plaster, finally painted with ashlar-joints in what is well-known to have been the 13th century fashion. The mouldings are closely datable, to c.1250. It is not known how many similarly deceptive works may exist in this stoneless county and what may be a rewarding line of research is suggested by this evidence.

Roofs

Most other examples of carpenters' structural work fall into three categories, the most impressive usually being the timber roof, or roofs, since large churches may have several of both ridged and lean-to types. Many Essex churches have been re-studied in the light of recent knowledge, but this limited text can do no more than describe a few. Even so, the choice is difficult because the county has such a wealth of examples.

The chancel roof of *Chipping Ongar* is probably the most rewarding, because the remains of three ancient systems survive there, supported by a dated seventeenth century system. From the chancel arch eastwards there are seven rafter-couples dating from the initial completion of the church during the late eleventh century. These rafter-couples are unique in this country. They form seven cants, and were jointed together by face pegs, without any form of tenons or integration of their component timbers. Similar roofs are recorded in France and Germany, but none of such early date.

A striking roof of the early fifteenth century is that over the nave of All Saints church at *Cressing,* probably dating from c.1425. This represents the general direction carpentered roofs had followed a little earlier in the cathedrals, such as over

44. *Blackmore. Most impressive of all Essex belfries.*

Fig. 2. *Sectioned scale drawing of the fifteenth century timber structure.*

45

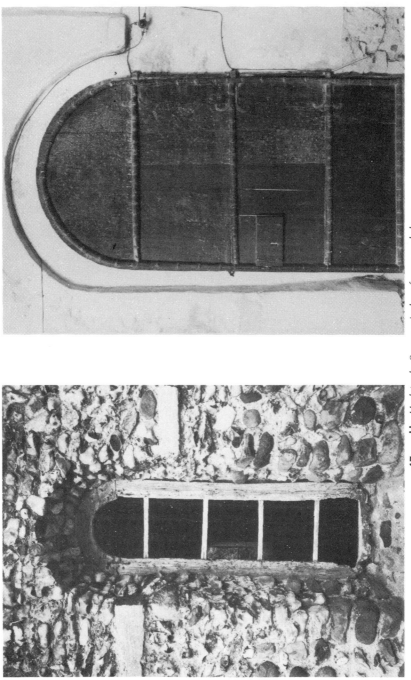

47a and b. *Hadstock. Saxon window frame and door.*

the presbytery of Winchester: various earlier designs were combined to form elaborate hybrids. This phase was the alternative to new designs, for which few possibilities remained. The Cressing example combined five distinct roof-types: tie-beamed, with wall-pieces and knees; arched braces to collars; crown-post with collar-purlin; side-purlins with in-pitch bracing; and common rafters framed into seven cants. A similarly complex roof exists at *Margaretting*, which combines three types.

Among the examples of the ultimate phase of roofing during the Perpendicular style are the various flat or camber-beamed roofs at *Saffron Walden* church. These are technically floors as much as roofs. The craftsmanship was lavished upon achieving richness of visual texture that conformed to the architectural style; while the emphasis upon grouped roll-mouldings on the chamfer planes induced the carpenters to adopt vee-sectioned timbers for either floors or roofs (they were little different) which were mechanically the weakest under loading and almost impossible to join together with strength. Even the elaborate hammer-beam roofs of *Castle Hedingham*, *Gestingthorpe* and *Great Bromley* are not as structurally sound as many earlier roofs.

Timbered towers

The timber towers, and western bell-turrets, both with their spires, have defied efforts at dating for a great many years; but they are datable if all the available evidence is assessed; two of the earliest surviving ones are of the greatest interest, and one of the latest serves to illustrate developments during the interim. Possibly the oldest is that at *Navestock* which was carbon dated: 1180±60. This was built around four cant-posts which were set-up at the same angle from vertical as the rafters of the spire, and these were surrounded by an outer wall, the whole stiffened by a series of lattice-like braces secured by notched lap-joints. The turret retains evidence of its original complement of three bells on an east-west axis, and a single soundvent in its west wall. The general style of this work is Early English, and the central carved oak boss of the visually simulated cross-vault inside illustrates the reference to local flora, similar to those in "The Leaves of Southwell Minster."

The small church, now remote from any settlement, at *Bradwell-juxta-Coggeshall*, is twelfth century and Norman; it has a western turret and spire of that period. The turret is framed with passing-braces forming a saltire in each wall, secured with notched lap-joints; but the original spire is now a matter for conjecture. At some date before 1320 when the murals were painted, the nave-walls were raised, the evidence of this is plainly visible from outside. This made the portal frame supporting the turret too short, and it was lengthened accordingly, leaving the two outside ends of its transverse beam protruding under the eaves, and exposing two chase-mortises for tenons with spurred shoulders—of the twelfth century—on the internal posts. These facts, together with the wall-paintings, make this as Sir Nikolaus Pevsner observed: "one of the essential ones to visit in Essex."

The best example of a late timber tower with spire is that at *Shenfield* church, built at the time when sound-vents were fitted continuously around all four walls of the turrets; this is likely to date during the last quarter of the fifteenth century. The evidence for this form of fenestration is only to be seen from the height of the turret, and the inside, but it was the ultimate type; designed to emit the sound of bells at their actual volume.

Porches

Porches do not have a very early origin, and the one ordered to be built for Henry III, in 1244 at Westminster Hall may indicate their beginnings, but if not, none have survived in Essex from before the fourteenth century. The south porch at *Bradwell-juxta-Coggeshall* is interesting in that it has scissor-braced rafters, placing its roof

47

typologically earlier than others in this county—the close of the thirteenth century being proposed for them. In addition this porch has tracery either side, of fourteenth century character; set upon turned balusters of late sixteenth century character. It is, therefore a highly instructive porch, and one that speaks of several styles and centuries.

More of a piece, and the most ambitious and splendid porch in the county, is that at *South Benfleet* church. This is Perpendicular in style, two bays in length, and fitted with a single hammerbeam roof. It has been spared from restorations, to date; and has superlative examples of side-light tracery, mullions, blind-tracery in its frontal spandrels and verge-boards. Considered as a complete timber building of two bays, it can be taken to illustrate everything that the wealthiest of clients could have requested for his residence during the fifteenth century.

A good example of the fifteenth century hybrids of structural types, is provided by the south porch at *West Hanningfield,* which combines collar-arched frames and spur-ties with side-purlins; this also has good side-light tracery. A representative of the Jacobean porch survives at *Mundon* church, where it must have been the most costly feature of that humble building, at the time of its construction; and the anomaly of a near contemporary porch at *Marks Tey* is that it may be defined as vernacular—being severe though sound, and fitted with stop-chamfered mullions, diamond-set.

Doors

Door-leaves are well represented in Essex parish churches; making a choice of exemplars difficult. The oldest two, in the present state of knowledge; are at *Hadstock* and *Buttsbury*. The first has been well known for centuries, and the second is a recent discovery comprising several successive and datable features. The north door at Hadstock is complete, but for a nineteenth century restoration, although hung in an opening proved to have been re-set, by archaeological examination. This leaf is of the round-headed Romanesque type, and has a rear-frame of almost circular ledges, of which the top one is bent to form; either by heating or steaming. The planks used are rebated, on the splay, and the whole is fastened with roves and clenches of iron; resembling the garboard strakes of a long ship of the period. The period concerned appears to be the opening of the eleventh century, when, as the Anglo Saxon Chronicle states: "in this year the King went to Assandun, and caused to be built there a monastery of stone and lime, for the souls of the men who were there slain, and gave it to one of his priests, whose name was Stigand" — and the year was A.D. 1020. There has been doubt as to the location of Assandun, but it is suggested that Hadstock was the region, the next village being Ashdon. The Buttsbury example is of the same construction, re-used by the Normans and covered with strap-ironwork of their period, and later re-cut and used in the essentially fourteenth century church there.

Of the great period, the Early English, Essex has an example, which, though small, displays much ingenuity. This is the south door of the church at *High Roding,* a masterly work of pure carpentry, to which the limited iron-work adds no more than hinges. It was framed with mortise and tenon joints, in such a way that its planks could be inserted from the base, between grooved edges; after which the bottom rail was fitted and pegged—the date may be c.1250. Of poorly constructed doors there is no shortage in any period, and it will be best to close with a good example from the Perpendicular: the south door of the church at *Tolleshunt D'Arcy.* This is, again, pure carpentry that relies upon no blacksmithed adjuncts for strength, it is fully framed like the previous specimen with good, planed mouldings on the muntins and durns (arches)—its planks being fitted into rebates from the rear.

THE PROGRESS OF BRICK

Christopher Starr

The unique and distinctive character of many Essex churches is largely due to the extensive and extremely varied use of either timber or brick in their construction.

Although they lacked suitable good-quality stone for building purposes, successive generations of Essex masons improvised with what they had—flint, puddingstone, septaria and ragstone. However, it was first with timber and then with brick—materials which, when needed, were never in short supply—that they were able to give expression to their innovative genius. We are fortunate that examples of their superb craftsmanship—particularly their wooden belfries and brick towers—have survived to the present day.

The first churches built in Essex, with the surviving exception of *St Peter's, Bradwell-on-Sea* which is almost wholly of Roman building materials, were mostly of timber. During the late Saxon and early Norman period many of these were replaced by stone structures and incorporated in the majority of them were Roman bricks, sometimes by the hundred.

When the Romans came to Essex they found not only an abundant supply of the clay essential for brick making, but also, in the forests, the necessary fuel. In the course of their four hundred year occupation they manufactured millions of bricks and tiles and a vast quantity of this durable material was available to their successors in the ruins of Colchester and many deserted villas.

Roman bricks clearly had a great appeal for both Saxon and Norman masons as they have been found in more than a hundred Essex churches of eleventh or twelfth century date. Sometimes it was for strength—as in the quoins at *Broomfield* and the tower stair newel at *Fyfield*; and sometimes for decoration—as in the chancel arch at *Great Hallingbury* and the doorways at *Wendens Ambo, Prittlewell* and *Holy Trinity Colchester*—that Roman bricks were used. There may even have been a superstitious need to include at least a fragment or two in every church building.

It is perhaps surprising that the technique of brickmaking had been unknown in England since the departure of the Romans in the fifth century, despite the fact that the tradition continued in France, Italy and elsewhere. It was probably monks of foreign origin building at *Little Coggeshall Priory* and *Waltham Abbey* in about 1170 who reintroduced bricks to England though it is thought possible that some of the bricks in *Copford* church may have been the result of earlier experiments to copy Roman brick—perhaps by an enterprising potter. Examples of the monks' large, rather thin bricks, sometimes termed "great bricks" have also been found in a number of other churches including *Danbury* and *West Bergholt*.

The next stage in the development of brickwork in Essex seems to have occurred in the fourteenth century and bricks of this date can be seen at *Dengie, Fordham, Purleigh* and *All Saints, Stanway*. Many of these bricks are pale yellow and appear either to have been manufactured in Essex by Flemings or imported from the Low Countries. At *Thorrington*, however, Roman bricks were still being used for decoration as late as c.1350 when the outer doorway of the porch was constructed.

From the fifteenth century, bricks began to be widely used for important secular purposes in Essex and a succession of manor houses—D'Arcy's Tower, Maldon (c.1435), Faulkbourne Hall (c.1440), Heron Hall, East Horndon (c.1460), Nether Hall, Roydon (c.1470)—were built. At *East Horndon* Sir Thomas Tyrell (who died in 1476), the builder of Heron Hall, had the old parish church pulled down and replaced by a building with a tower, nave, chancel and two transepts all of brick. He referred to this act of piety in his Will "I will that if I make not up in my lifetime the steeple and new work which I have begun at East Horndon .... then my executors (shall) see that it may be made up and done." A brick porch and south chapel were added to the church by his successors.

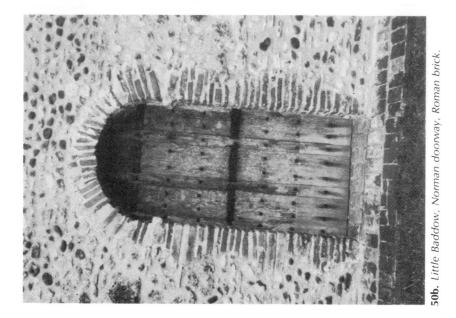

50b. *Little Baddow, Norman doorway, Roman brick.*

50a. *Heybridge, variety of material in Norman wall.*

It may be that other major church construction work was undertaken in brick at the end of the fifteenth century and much research needs to be done before a complete picture emerges. Save for a few exceptions, the majority of surviving early brickwork in Essex churches cannot be dated with precision and it may be that much of it will eventually prove to be older than is presently thought.

Whereas *East Horndon*, then *Layer Marney* and *Chignal Smealy* were rebuilt almost entirely of brick (as was the tiny chapel of c. 1490 at *Great Horkesley*) it was more usual in Tudor Essex for brick additions or repairs to be made to existing churches—most commonly towers, porches and chapels. About thirty brick towers were built in Essex between 1500 and 1530—*Wickham St Paul* can be fairly precisely dated to 1505 and *Theydon Garnon* to 1520—these towers are massive, often tall with three or four stages, usually the bricks are dark red and patterned with a decoration of bluish bricks called diaper work. There are stepped battlements, pinnacles and a stair turret rising above them from the angle of two of the walls. There may also be a west doorway with a lofty, rather wide window above it. These towers are usually strengthened by a number of slim, stepped diagonal buttresses. Perhaps the most splendid of these are to be seen at *Ingatestone, Rochford, Layer Marney, Rayne, Sandon* and *Fryerning* but *Downham, Billericay, Castle Hedingham, Liston, Tilbury-juxta-Clare, Ugley, Nazeing* and *Gestingthorpe* are all worth a visit. *Weeley* is interesting for the curiously large bricks which make up the lowest three metres of the tower. It is not unusual to find that Essex towers faced with stone have a Tudor brick core—as at *Chelmsford Cathedral* and *Danbury*.

Brick porches built on the south side of churches during the early Tudor period can be seen all over Essex but notably at *Stambourne, Sturmer, Elsenham, East Horndon, Little Sampford, Sandon, Pebmarsh, Feering, High Easter, Great Henny* and *Lamarsh*. North porches of brick are rare; there is one at *West Mersea* of Tudor date and another at *Wethersfield* of c.1750. The window sills in the porch at *Castle Hedingham* form seats and at *Great Yeldham*, an upper room and gable were added in brick to the earlier porch.

Stone towers were sometimes repaired or heightened with brick during the sixteenth century as at *Little Bromley, Sheering, Boxted, Springfield* and *Tollesbury*.

Occasionally, as at *Ashen, Hatfield Peverel* and *Finchingfield* a brick stair turret was added; or a turret topped with brick as at *Belchamp Walter*, whilst at *Great Sampford* a brick staircase with oak treads was built inside the tower. More frequently, the walls of tower, nave or chancel were repaired or buttressed with brick at this time, for example, at *Ashingdon, Great Maplestead, Peldon, Tolleshunt Knights* and *Dedham*. Also in the sixteenth century a number of chancels were built entirely in brick including *Greensted, Little Warley, Langley* and *Basildon* whilst others, like *Hempstead*, were merely repaired with brick.

From c.1510 brick chantry or manorial chapels were popular. One of the first was the Tyrell family's chapel at *East Horndon*, followed by the chapels of the Marneys at *Layer Marney*, the Petres at *Ingatestone* and the Audleys at *Berechurch*. Similar brick chapels may also be found at *West Ham, Latton* and *Kelvedon*.

Many other examples of Tudor brickwork are to be seen in Essex churches—at *Castle Hedingham* and *Great Baddow* a clerestory, at *Stow Maries* a corbel table, at *Little Bromley* a brick aisle, at *St Osyth* and *Blackmore* the nave arcades are brick and at *Latton* so is the rood doorway. Brick window openings and tracery are also widespread and are to be found at *Berners Roding, North Benfleet, Little Burstead, Chignal St James* and *Mount Bures*. At *Coggeshall* there is an underground sacristy and at *East Horndon* a vaulted crypt—neither of which is now accessible however. Occasionally brick fittings can also be found—there is a brick font at *Chignal Smealy* and canopied brick niches on either side of the nave at *Tolleshunt Major*. By the mid-sixteenth century the use of brick in churches was virtually confined to repairs but in 1563-64 the only church to be built in Essex during the reign of Elizabeth I was constructed entirely of brick at *Woodham Walter*.

During the seventeenth century the use of brick revived—towers were built at

52a. *Thorrington, Roman brick utilised c.1350.*

52b. *Dengie, pale yellow 14th century bricks.*

Towers. 53a. *Layer Marney c.1520*

53b. *Fryerning c. 1525.*

Porches. 53c. *Feering c.1525*

53d. *Theydon Mount c. 1615.*

Castle Hedingham (1616), *Leyton* (1658)—the only substantial example of Cromwellian church architecture in the county—*Stansted* (1692) and *Toppesfield* (1699), there is a seventeenth century brick porch at *Little Sampford* and a complete brick church at *Theydon Mount*. The early eighteenth century produced some fine brick towers—*Bradwell-on-Sea* (1706), *Woodford* (1708), *Little Warley* (1718) and *Terling* (1732) and several churches completely of brick—*Ingrave, Wanstead, North Fambridge* and *Shellow Bowells*. This tradition continued well into the nineteenth century with brick towers at *Bobbingworth, High Ongar, Harwich, Helions Bumpstead, Messing* and *Stapleford Abbots,* and the churches at *Twinstead, Abridge* and *East Donyland* are all of brick.

MONUMENTAL BRASSES

Nancy Briggs

Essex is an interesting county for the student of brasses. With nearly 300 surviving figure brasses, it is comparable with Norfolk, Suffolk and Kent.

The finest of the three Essex military brasses dating from the first half of the 14th century is at *Pebmarsh*. Sir William Fitz Ralph, who died between 1331 and 1338, is shown almost life-size wearing a linen surcoat over chain mail, with plate defences for the arms, legs and feet.

The small Flemish figure plate of Sir Ralph de Knevynton (d.1370) at *Aveley*, with its use of dating by the dominical letter in the inscription of English workmanship, is a complete contrast to the large composition with triple canopy commemorating Sir John de la Pole and his wife Joan Cobham at *Chrishall*, c.1380; the couple are shown holding hands.

Another fine canopied brass at *Little Horkesley* commemorates a father and son, Sir Robert Swynborne (d.1391) and Sir Thomas Swynborne (d.1412); Sir Robert in aventail and jupon is deliberately portrayed in late 14th century armour. The Swynborne brasses and that commemorating Dame Bridget Marnay (d.1549) shown with her two husbands all in heraldic dress, were saved when the church was completely demolished by enemy action in 1940.

The brass of Henry Bourchier, 1st Earl of Essex (d.1483), in Garter robes, and his Countess, Isabel Plantagenet, both wearing collars of Suns and Roses, was moved at the Dissolution from Beeleigh Abbey to *Little Easton*.

Two unusually large and fine 16th century compositions at *Wivenhoe* commemorate William, Viscount Beaumont (d.1507) and his widow, Elizabeth, Countess of Oxford (d.1537). Viscount Beaumont's brass has a wealth of detail, with the elephant and castle at his feet echoed in the spandrels of the canopy and the stops of the marginal inscription. The Countess wears a coronet and heraldic mantle.

Heraldic dress also features on the brass of Sir Richard FitzLewes (d.1528) and his four wives at *Ingrave*.

Priests were normally commemorated by smaller brasses than the landed classes. There are good 14th century half-effigies at *Corringham* (Richard de Beltoun, c.1340) and *Stifford* (Ralph Perchehay, d.1378). An unusually large and fine 15th century example at *Great Bromley* shows William Byschopton (d.1432) in mass vestments under a canopy. William Kyrkeby at *Theydon Garnon* (d.1458) is also large and is the only surviving Essex example wearing a cope. The finest Essex ecclesiastical brass is that to Archbishop Samuel Harsnett (d.1631) at *Chigwell*, where he was once vicar; the brass, probably designed by the sculptor, Edward Marshall, can hardly be other than a portrait of the Archbishop, with his large hooked nose; he is shown in cope with mitre and crosier.

Fifteenth century lawyers are well represented. The earliest is Thomas Rolf, Serjeant-at-Law (d.1440) at *Gosfield*, with an eulogistic inscription in Latin verse hardly in accord with the turbulent career of this "flower among lawyers." Sir Peter Arderne, Chief Baron of the Exchequer (d.1465) lies with his wife on the altar tomb in the chantry at *Latton* which he founded, near the brass of his daughter and her husband, Richard Harper (d.1492). Both Harper and Sir Thomas Urswyk, Chief Baron of the Exchequer (d.1479), were associated with Arderne's chantry. Urswyk's own brass at *Dagenham* shows him with his wife, in a butterfly head-dress, and a group of 9 daughters, the eldest a nun at Barking, and the younger girls in curious steeple head-dresses.

Most of these large and elaborate compostions to members of the wealthier classes were made in London workshops, but N.W. Essex has a number of brasses, c.1515 — c.1530, commissioned by members of the middle class, and almost certainly made at Cambridge. Characteristic and closely related examples c. 1530 are found at *Elmdon*

Fig. 3. *Little Horkesley.*
Sir Robert Swynborne (1391) and
Sir Thomas Swynborne (1412).

Fig. 4. *Elmdon.*
Civilian and family, c.1530.

Within this pit of Terling is entered an Esquier
Whose lyfe to vertues path was bente, till death dyde claime his hire
His name hyght William Rochester, With whom lyeth buried here
Elizabeth his only wyfe, a loving faythfull fere
The fatall darte of pepinge death, hir lyfe dyde take away
In July mounth departed sher, the nyne and twenty day
A thousand & fyue hundreth yeres, from Christ his incarnacon
And fyftie fyue the truth to showe, as fayne will make relacion
This worthy gentleman not longe, he hynde his loving wyfe
The seconde of September dyde, yelde vp his mortall lyfe
In anno as I sayd before, of hundred fyue tymes three
And three & eyght his soule dyde goe where all good chosen bee

Fig. 5. *Terling. William Rochester and family, 1558.*

Fig. 6. *Chigwell. Samuel Harsnett, Archbishop of York, 1631.*

and *Saffron Walden;* the former consists of a civilian and two wives, groups of children on rectangular plates, with a marginal inscription. The women at Elmdon and Saffron Walden are shown wearing tam o' shanters, shoulder capes, and sashes with trifoliate clasps; the men, with distinctive hair-styles and fur-edged gowns, are standing upon tiled floors.

The 16th century brasses of the Darcy family, now mural in the Darcy chapel at *Tolleshunt D'Arcy,* include the curious large figure in armour of Anthony Darcy (d.1540) almost certainly a piece of local workmanship modelled on the brass in the same church of John de Boys, c.1420. The discovery of the slab in 1977 revealed that Anthony Darcy's brass was surrounded by a late 14th century Flemish marginal inscription, of which one fragment survives. The design consists of a vine scroll with the Virgin and Child in the centre, the emblems of St Luke and St Mark, and the clauses of the Apostle's Creed associated with St Philip and St Bartholomew, shown seated.

Fig. 7. *Tolleshunt Darcy. Flemish fragment, c.1375.*

London-made brasses predominate once again during the Elizabethan Revival, some of the finer examples being ascribed to the Southwark workshops. Family groups kneeling at faldstools closely parallel Elizabethan wall monuments, especially when the brass is set in a stone frame. Two generations of the Rochester family are commemorated in this way in the south aisle at *Terling.* William Rochester (d.1558) erected c.1570, has round arches over each group of kneeling figures; a similar composition in a simpler frame commemorates his son, John (d.1584).

Some late Elizabethan and early Jacobean brasses may have been designed by Gerard Johnson. William Golding (d.1587) at *Belchamp St Paul,* is an armoured figure of high quality, standing on a tiled floor. Civilians and ladies associated with this workshop are usually shown standing on circular hassocks, an early example being Joan Rysbye (d.1598) at *Bradfield.* Ann Thompson, who died in childbirth in 1607, aged 31, is shown at *Berden* with her husband, 9 sons and 7 daughters.

Twelve other churches to visit; *Barking, Bocking, Bowers Gifford, Brightlingsea, Coggeshall, Halstead, Harlow, Hempstead, Hornchurch, Roydon, Upminster, Writtle.*

MONUMENTS

A.C. Edwards

Development

In Essex, as in other counties, the evolution of church monuments with effigies came late and proceeded slowly. It seems to have begun with the lids of stone coffins. Ninety-six of these lids survive in Essex, and of these some 58 belong to the 13th century. Most of them bore a carved stone cross; on three of them, all much mutilated, the figure of a knight is carved in low relief. The oldest, found in a rockery at Colne Priory, depicts Aubrey de Vere, d.1141, the builder of Hedingham Castle keep; the other two, of the mid-13th century, are at *Faulkbourne* and *Toppesfield*.

These three knights are on coffin lids of tapering English shape. By the early 13th century a new stage was developing; stone effigies in full relief on rectangular slabs which were never coffin lids but might well have been placed *over* stone coffins buried below church floors. An interesting example is of Robert de Vere, 3rd Earl of Oxford, at *Hatfield Broad Oak*. He died in 1221 but his cross-legged effigy in clunch was carved somewhat later; the figure is much worn but was originally of high quality. Sometimes, as at *Clavering*, an effigy with its slab was placed at floor level in a low recess cut in a church wall. Sometimes, the recesses were elaborately decorated, like the Bouteton monument, 1325, at *Belchamp Walter*, with its carved cusps, finials and heraldry.

It was not long before the rectangular base-slab developed into the chest tomb, with its sides panelled or given canopied recesses with small effigies of angels or 'weepers.' Sometimes a chest tomb was left free-standing in the body of a church, as with the monument to Sir William Marney at *Layer Marney*. Sometimes, it was placed against a wall; it could then be given a carved backplate, as with the Lovaine monument, c.1400, at *Little Easton*. Occasionally, it was given a full canopy, like a four-poster bed; a good example is the monument to Henry Bouchier, Earl of Essex, 1483, also at Little Easton. The tomb chest, in various forms, continued into Tudor and Stuart times. One of the most notable in the county commemorates Henry, Lord Marney, 1523, at *Layer Marney*. Here the chest and canopy are of terra cotta, while the effigy is of black Catacleuse stone.

Considerable change in the development of monuments came with the Reformation and through Renaissance influence. There was a deeper obsession with death, and this is seen in the use of carved emblems of mortality—skulls, complete skeletons, bones, hourglasses, scythes. Yet, curiously, there was a greater mobility in the effigies themselves. Often they are no longer in the posture of death; they begin to wake up; they lie uncomfortably on their sides; they kneel; later, they recline gracefully, they sit up; they stand up; in some of the group monuments standing figures are almost like conversation pieces.

While tomb chests with their effigies continued into Tudor and Stuart times, the wall monument became increasingly popular. The standard type showed kneeling effigies of husband and wife facing one another across a prayer desk, with their kneeling children ranged behind them. A charming variant is the monument to Cecily Sandys, d.1610, wife of Archbishop Sandys, at *Woodham Ferrers*. Her figure kneels at a *prie-dieu* between two Corinthian pillars; the back of the monument and the rounded arch above are carved in trellis work with flowers and foliage—almost a pleached arbour.

In the 17th century, a new type of monument became popular, the frontal demi-figure. Perhaps the best of these is the Merry monument, 1633, at *Walthamstow*. Here, Nicholas Stone depicts Sir Thomas and Lady Merry, each in an oval niche. In the same year, 1633, at *Abbess Roding*, Stone's contemporary, Epiphanius Evesham, shows two cherubs holding back curtains to reveal Lady Luckyn's demi-effigy. Later, the bust replaced the demi-figure. The most notable is by Edward Marshall at

60a. *Little Baddow. Oak effigy of a man c.1320.*

60b. *Little Dunmow. Alabaster effigies of Walter Fitzwalter (1432) and his wife (1464).*

Hempstead. It commemorates the famous physician, William Harvey, 1657. At *Writtle*, a later monument by Sir Henry Cheere, shows the bust of Sir John Comyns, 1740, on a marble sarcophagus.

The best reclining effigy of the 17th century is that of Richard, Lord Rich (d. 1568, but monument erected c.1620) at *Felsted*. But it is in Georgian times that this type of monument reaches the height of elegance, as at *Steeple Bumpstead*. Here, beneath an enriched pediment supported by twisted, barley-sugar columns, the effigy of Sir Henry Bendyshe, 1717, reclines most gracefully, his right elbow resting on a cushion and his right hand supporting his chin.

Georgian monuments with standing figures seem to typify the self-satisfaction of that age. At *Rettendon* a remarkable and little-known example commemorates Edmund Humphrey, 1727, and his friends. Behind and above the main, semi-reclining figure, four others stand in niches beneath a pediment. Almost equally striking is Charles Stanley's vast monument to Lord Maynard, 1746, at *Little Easton*. Maynard's figure stands on a pedestal halfway up the monument; around him are members of his family shown as busts or on medallions.

Many post-medieval monuments, especially from the 17th century onwards, bear interesting inscriptions. A heraldic ledger floorslab in *Blackmore* church was laid down to the memory of a Royalist rector, Simon Lynch, "who for fearing God and the King was sequestered, prosecuted and persecuted by Gog and Magog." A wall monument at *Lambourne* commemorates Captain George Lockwood, slain in the charge of the Light Brigade at Balaclava. At *Gestingthorpe* there is an inscription to 'a very gallant gentleman', Captain Laurence Oates, 1912, one of Scott's companions on that tragic South Pole expedition, who 'being gravely injured, went out into the blizzard to die, in the hope that by so doing he might enable his comrades to reach safety.'

Distribution and Quality
Except in times of disaster, such as the Black Death of 1348 and the Great Depression of the late 19th century, Essex has always been a rich farming county, with an assured and expanding market in the Capital; and from the late Middle Ages to the 18th century its agricultural wealth was supplemented by the cloth trade. This wealth is reflected in its church monuments. They are widely distributed throughout the county. Over forty churches are worth visiting for their monuments, and of these the following are outstanding: *Danbury* (oak effigies); *Hempstead* (Harvey family; also brasses); *Ingatestone* (Petre family); *Lambourne* (Lockwood family); *Layer Marney* (Marney family); *Little Baddow* (oak effigies; Mildmay monument), *Little Dunmow* (Fitzwalter family); *Little Easton* (Lovaine, Bourchier and Maynard families); *Little Horkesley* (oak effigies; also brasses); *Rettendon*; *Steeple Bumpstead*; *Theydon Mount* (Smith family); *Writtle* (various monuments; also brasses).

The quality of Essex monuments varies considerably. None is of outstanding national importance, such as the Royal effigies in Westminster Abbey or the superb latten monument to Richard Beauchamp, Earl of Warwick, 1439, in St Mary's church, Warwick. A number of Essex examples, especially some Georgian effigies, are executed with considerable skill. Numerous important sculptors are represented: Nicholas Stone (*Walthamstow, Writtle*); Epiphanius Evesham (*Felsted, Abbess Roding, Ingatestone, Stansted Mountfitchet*); Edward Marshall (*Hempstead*); Thomas Stayner (*Steeple Bumpstead*); John Nost (*Dagenham, Wanstead*); Louis Roubilliac (*Barking*); J.M. Rysbrack (*Gosfield*); Peter Scheemakers (*Faulkbourne*); Sir Henry Cheere (*Barking, Writtle, Pleshey*); John Flaxman (*Hornchurch, Hatfield Broad Oak, Leyton, Lambourne*); Sir Francis Chantrey (*Wanstead, Bradfield*). Rossi, the two Bacons, Nollekens and Westmacott are also represented.

Three Essex churches above all others should be visited. There are ten oaken effigies in the county; the two at *Little Baddow* are of exceptional quality. They are of a man in civilian dress, c.1340, and his wife, each in its own canopied recess. The

61

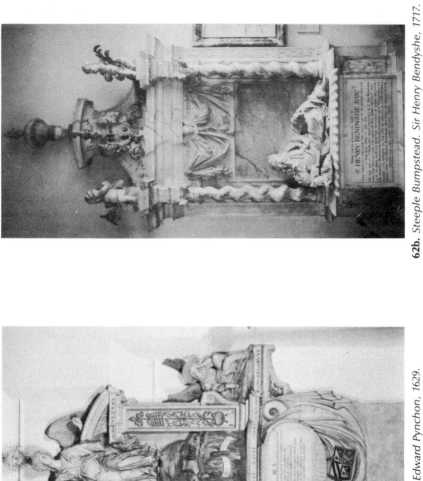

62b. *Steeple Bumpstead. Sir Henry Bendyshe, 1717.*

62a. *Writtle. Sir Edward Pynchon, 1629.*

sculptor chose a bent oak trunk for the lady; thus the figure is most delicately curved. The head of the man is exquisitively carved in relation to the grain. They and the alabaster Fitzwalter figures, c.1460, in *Little Dunmow* church display a tranquillity which is rarely seen in later memorial sculpture; it is as if they were content to say 'Amen'.

The third church, *Writtle*, has a standing wall monument of quite a different order. It commemorates Sir Edward Pynchen, and was erected in 1629 by Nicholas Stone at a cost of £66.13s.4d. It is a superb allegory: beneath the sun, the figure of an angel reaper, once holding a scythe, now lost; the sheaves below; the trophies of agricultural implements; the mourning angels with wide-brimmed harvesters' hats; the winnowing fan holding the inscription; the corn shovel, bearing the coat of arms. It reflects the spirit of that age — that golden melancholy with which Shakespeare and others sought to invest the mystery of death. After all, Nicholas Stone, working on the South Bank, probably knew Shakespeare. He may have seen the masquers in *The Tempest*. He may well have heard the words of *Fidele* in *Cymbeline*.

FUNERAL HATCHMENTS

C. Harrold

In the parish churches of Essex we have one of the largest collections of funeral hatchments in the country—over two hundred in fact, and together they represent a form of personal memorial which is part of Britain's heraldic tradition.

Originating in the Low Countries in the seventeenth century, the hatchment evolved from the medieval "achievement"—the shield, helm, sword and other accoutrements carried at a knight's funeral and, as at *Bradfield*, deposited in the church above his tomb. In England, it became customary for the hatchment with the deceased's coat of arms surrounded by a black background to be painted on canvas stretched over a lozenge-shaped frame. This was hung outside his house during the period of mourning and thereafter in the parish church.

In Essex, the development of the hatchment from the "achievement"—through the transitional stage of armorial panel—to the lozenge shape with its distinctive background—can be traced in a number of churches. An interesting example being at *Pebmarsh* where there is both an armorial panel and a hatchment-type painting mounted lozengewise. This is blazoned—that is to say described in heraldic language, as sable, three bendlets argent (Cooke) impaling argent, on a chief gules, two molets or (St John). There is an inscription to Judith, wife of Thomas Cooke, daghter of Oliver St John, who was buried 7 April 1674 and her husband on 4 March 1680.

Several of the earliest examples of funeral hatchments having the distinctive background can be seen at *Chigwell* where, like many seventeenth century hatchments, they are about two feet square. The special significance of the background is that it indicates the sex and marital state of the deceased. The heraldic description of the coat of arms on a hatchment is made as if one were holding the shield, the dexter side being the right hand as one holds it or the left hand as one looks at it. Heraldic usage dictates that the dexter side refers to a man and the sinister side to a woman when it is necessary to distinguish between them.

At *Messing* there is a hatchment showing a shield with helm and crest whose dexter background is black thus indicating that the deceased is a man who is survived by his wife. The coat of arms is blazoned as follows: sable, a fess dancetty between two leopards' faces or, the badge of Ulster (Luckyn) impaling argent, on a fess sable, three molets or and in dexter chief an ermine spot (Grimston). For the crest, out of a tower chequy or and sable a demigriffin or. The hatchment commemorates Sir Capell Luckyn, the 2nd baronet, of Messing Hall, who in 1648 married Mary, daughter of Sir Harbottle Grimston of Bradfield. Sir Capell died in 1680, his widow in 1718. Her hatchment has the same arms without a crest and is depicted on a lozenge, it has an all black background indicating that she was a widow. A lozenge, rather than a shield, is used on hatchments to depict the arms of a lady. In the same church is a hatchment which shows only the Luckyn arms (with the badge of Ulster to indicate a baronet) on an all black background, indicating that the deceased was a batchelor. He was, in fact, Sir Harbottle Luckyn, the 4th Baronet, who died unmarried in 1736.

If the background of the sinister side of the shield is black, and the coat of arms is shown on a shield rather than a lozenge, this is the hatchment of a married woman whose husband has survived her. An example is in *Holy Trinity, Colchester*, where one of the five hatchments which were restored by Mr. J. Robinson has a sinister black background. The coat of arms is sable, a chevron wavy between three eagles displayed or (Shawe) impaling sable, a chevron between three trefoils slipped argent (Lewis). The crest is a hart's head transfixed through the head by an arrow proper. This is for Thamar, daughter of Samuel Lewis of Roydon, Suffolk, who married Sir John Shawe, Recorder of Colchester and died in 1681. Her husband's hatchment has the same arms on an all black background because, when he died in 1690, he was a widower.

65a. *Gosfield. Widower. James Goodeve Sparrow, 1838.*

65b. *High Ongar. Married man survived by wife.*
Revd. John Bramston-Stane, 1857.

65

A spinster's hatchment shows a single coat of arms rather than an impaled coat on a lozenge with an all black background and one of these is in *Henham* church. It is one of the four restored by Mr. E.B.A. Everett and has on it a lozenge, surmounted by a cherub's head, the arms of Feake—sable, a fess dancetty or, in chief three fleur-de-lis argent. This is for Mary Feake who died in 1803, the daughter and co-heiress of Samuel Feake.

In Essex there are examples of the several ways in which a hatchment can represent a dead man with two wives. One is at *Chigwell* in memory of Thomas Scott of Woolston Hall who died in 1732. One of his two wives predeceased him as can be seen from the backgrounds. His arms, per pale indented argent and sable, a sattire countercharged, are on the centre shield and they are flanked by two other shields. The shield to the dexter of the main shield (Scott impaling or, two bars and a chief indented gules) has an all black background but the small shield to the sinister (Scott impaling sable, a chevron between three roses argent each charged with a saltire sable) has a dexter black background. This indicates the widowed second wife.

There is a hatchment in the vestry at *Great Horkesley* which, despite having a black background on the sinister or female side, is for a man—it is, in fact, the hatchment of a Bishop. Since his See survives him, the See's arms are always depicted in the dexter side of a Bishop's coat of arms. The Rt. Revd. William Ward D.D. who died in 1838, was rector of Great Horkesley and subsequently Bishop of Sodor and Man. The three legs in armour of the See of Man occupy the dexter side and instead of a helmet and crest is a bishop's mitre.

The largest collection of hatchments in Essex is at *Chigwell* where there are seventeen. *Orsett* has fourteen, of which thirteen are in the Whitmore chapel. Whereas Chigwell has the oldest, Orsett has one of the most modern funeral hatchments in the county. This is for Violet Elizabeth, the daughter of Sir William Houldsworth. She married Col. Sir Francis Whitmore in 1900 and died in 1927. The coat of arms was painted by Sir Francis himself and shows vert, fretty or (Whitmore) impaling ermine, a tree trunk in bend eradicated proper between three foxes' heads gules (Houldsworth). The background is all black but strictly speaking it should be sinister black. On hatchments it is not unusual for the heraldry and background to be incorrect.

At *Great Baddow* there are hatchments to two eighteenth century members of the Hawker family. The arms depict a hawk proper, jessed and belled upon a perch or. This is an example of canting arms—the bird being a pun on the family name. *Theydon Mount* has a series of hatchments to members of the Smyth family, their crest being a salamander in flames reguardant proper, ducally gorged or and their coat of arms shows an altar flaming proper. On one of them is, in pretence (a coat of arms in the centre of the shield), three demi-woodmen each holding in the dexter hand over the dexter shoulder a club proper; this is for the Wood family.

Ramsey church has a striking coat of arms in the hatchment of Lieutenant General Burr. The hatchment is dexter black so clearly he was survived by his wife whose coat of arms is in pretence. Arms so placed indicate that she was an heraldic heiress, that is, her family was armigerous and she had no surviving brothers. In fact, she was the daughter and co-heiress of James Davis of Chepstow and co-heiress of Frances, late Dowager Duchess of Norfolk. As well as indicating the General's wife Mary Davis, the arms show that his mother Elizabeth was daughter and heiress of John Davall. We know this because the Davall arms appear in the second and third quarters of the main shield.

For many of us, the pleasure we get from looking at a hatchment is in the colour and artistic effect. Unfortunately, however, many of them are hidden away and hard to see clearly. A useful tip when hatchment hunting is to take a pair of binoculars and a good torch. Although some hatchments have been, and are being, expertly restored—for example those by Mr. and Mrs. K.R. Mabbitt at *St James', Colchester*,

67a. *Ramsey.*
Married man survived by wife.
Lt. Gen. Daniel Burr, 1828.

67b. *Birdbrook.*
Bachelor and last of his line.
Thomas Walford D. L., 1833.

67c. *Ramsey.*
Detail from above showing wife's arms
"in pretence".

Stanford-le-Hope, Great Baddow and *Great Waltham*—many of these interesting heraldic and genealogical signposts to the past are still neglected. It is hoped that efforts will be made to preserve these hatchments before they are irretrievably lost. Further examples of Essex funeral hatchments may be seen at *Canewdon, Sutton, Boreham, Paglesham, Strethall, Little Sampford, Great Easton, Pentlow, Black Notley* and *Bobbingworth*.

ROYAL ARMS

Rosemary Pardoe

Royal Arms have been placed in churches since the Reformation as symbols of the monarch's Headship of the Church of England. There are examples predating 1534 but these are clearly just for decoration, mainly in stained glass. At one time, about the end of the eighteenth century, almost all churches possessed a set of Royal Arms. Unfortunately many were lost during nineteenth century restorations, and now only the minority of parishes still retain these Coats of Arms.

Royal achievements prior to 1649 are now rare because they were mostly removed during the Commonwealth. Essex contains at least four examples, of which the earliest is probably the well-known carving at *Waltham Abbey*, which depicts the Tudor arms (Quarterly the arms of France and England; 1st and 4th, three gold fleurs-de-lys on blue; 2nd and 3rd, three gold passant lions on red) supported by a gilded lion and dragon. In 1821 it was seen by T. Willement who described it in his *Regal Heraldry* as having an inscription, "5 P. & M. 1558". This has led to the belief that the arms are those of the first Queen Mary (1553-8), which would make them unique in a church, as Mary discouraged the practice. It does seem likely, however, that the inscription was a later addition and that the arms are in fact of Elizabeth I (1558-1603).

The second Elizabeth I achievement in Essex is much less well known, but just as good a carving. It is at *Middleton* and is a nicely decorated, unpainted, wood set in half relief.

Moving on to the early Stuarts, *Theydon Bois* has a painting with the Stuart arms (Quarterly; 1st and 4th the Tudor arms; 2nd the arms of Scotland, a red rampant lion on gold with a double border; 3rd the arms of Ireland, a gold harp on blue), supported by the lion and unicorn which have flanked the Royal shield since 1603. Above the supporters are the initals "I.R." for "Iacobus Rex", and since the arms are believed to date from 1618 they must be those of James I. They have been restored quite recently and are in fine condition.

At *Messing* is a carved and painted achievement from the reign of Charles I (1625-49). It is a very striking piece of work, in excellent condition, and dated "1634". What makes it particularly rare is that the Prince of Wales' Feathers are painted on the reverse. Although churches were encouraged to erect these symbols along with the King's Arms in the seventeenth century, only a few remain today.

During the Commonwealth (1649-60) the Royal Arms were taken down and Commonwealth Arms put up in their place. Only one set from this period remains in a church; at *North Walsham* in Norfolk; but another was discovered on a piece of plaster during the demolition of *Hazeleigh* church in 1922. Unfortunately it could not be saved.

At the Restoration of Charles II in 1660 it was naturally ordered that the Commonwealth Arms should be removed from all buildings, and the King's Arms erected to replace them. This probably accounts for the large number of achievements dating from 1660 still to be found in our churches. Essex has examples at *Finchingfield*, *Great Baddow*, *Langdon Hills*, *Langham*, *Little Easton*, *Saffron Walden*, *White Notley* and *Woodham Walter*. Especially worthy of mention is the one at *Langdon Hills*. That church is now a private dwelling house, but according to a photograph in *The Times* 16/8/76 the owner has retained the Royal Arms (which are painted onto the plaster of the tympanum). Most undated Carolean achievements (such as the good painting at *Shenfield*) probably also date from the 1660's.

The short reign of James II (1685-8) produced a surprising number of Royal Arms. Essex has two, at *Ashingdon* and *Rivenhall*, both of which were made after the Archdeacon's Visitation of 1684-5 directed that they be obtained.

The Arms of William III and Mary (1689-1702) were Stuart with the addition of an inescutcheon of Nassau: A gold rampant lion on a blue background sown with gold

70a. *Shenfield. Stuart 1603-1688.*

70b. *Asheldham. Hanover 1801-1816.*

70c. *Woodham Ferrers. Hanover 1714-1801.*

70d. *West Tilbury. Hanover 1801-1816.*

71b. *Hadstock. Hanover 1714-1801.*

71d. *Stapleford Tawney. Hanover 1816-1837.*

71a. *Bradwell-on-Sea. Hanover 1714-1801.*

71c. *Great Tey. Hanover 1816-1837.*

71

72. *All Saints, Maldon. Stuart 1603-1688.*

billets. *Witham* and *Sible Hedingham* have two fine carvings of this date, both with the distinctive motto of William III: "Ie Main Tien (or Tain) Dray" (Je Maintaindrai). *Colchester St Peter* has a rare and unusual carving from this time. The heraldry on the shield is: Quarterly; 1st England; 2nd Scotland; 3rd Ireland; 4th France; with the Nassau inescutcheon. This simplified version of the Royal Arms also appeared on half crown coins at the beginning of the period.

From 1702 to 1707 Queen Anne bore the Stuart arms, and the best Essex example from this time is at *Thaxted*, painted on wood cut to the shape of the arms. It has Queen Anne's motto, "Semper Eadem". After the Union with Scotland, until her death in 1714, Queen Anne's arms were as follows: Quarterly; 1st and 4th England impaling Scotland; 2nd France; 3rd Ireland. *Hadleigh* has a good set as does the *Black Chapel* at *North End*. Unfortunately the painting at *Kelvedon* has been damaged by having holes pushed through it to make way for bell rope holders.

From 1714 to 1837 the Hanoverian Kings ruled, and the complex arms of Hanover (including the Westphalian White Horse) appeared in the British Royal Arms. They were placed in the fourth quarter of the shield until 1801 when they were moved into an inescutcheon topped by an Electoral Bonnet until 1816, and by a Crown from 1816 to 1837. Except for the inescutcheon the arms were, from 1801, as we know them today: Quarterly; 1st and 4th England; 2nd Scotland; 3rd Ireland. It would be quite impossible to list all of the Essex examples from this period; there are well over seventy; but the 1715 painting at *Horndon-on-the-Hill* should be mentioned as it is signed by "William Waite of Gravesend"; probably the only signed set in Essex. Dating from 1816-37 are cast iron achievements in fifteen Essex churches (for instance *Birdbrook, Mistley, Great Tey*). These were all made by Wallis and Coleman who had an ironfoundry in Colchester.

The modern Royal Coat which came into use with Queen Victoria in 1837 can only be seen in a few Essex churches, as the tradition of erecting the arms had begun to die out by then. Two identical and charming metalwork sets are at *Elmdon* and *Mucking*. At *Sturmer* is a very curious example of updating; the shield contains the modern arms, but the initials are "G.2d.R". The opposite occurs at *Great Burstead* where the 1714-1801 arms have the initials "V.R.".

The most recent Royal achievement in this county is at *St Paul's Harlow* and dates from the church's completion in 1959. While it is good to see the tradition continuing, it is surely more important to retain and restore the existing work. H. & K. Mabbitt of Colchester have done much sensitive restoration work on Royal Arms in Essex, most notably at *Messing, West Mersea, Hadleigh* and on several of the metalwork examples. Restoration should never be left to local amateurs who can do more harm than good. At *North Fambridge*, for instance, the 1764 arms have recently been completely repainted, leaving no trace of the original and making a mockery of the heraldry. Repainting is seldom necessary; cleaning and a little retouching can usually make a startling difference provided deterioration is not too severe.

Grants are available for the restoration of the older and more interesting Royal achievements and there can be no excuse at all for their loss. There was also no excuse for the ruin of the attractive Hanoverian arms at *Asheldham* which were left to the elements and the birds when that church became redundant.

Essex has a good selection of Royal Arms in its churches, mostly in good or adequate condition, but some in need of treatment. The Hanoverian examples seem to suffer most from this. Although they may be quite common, some are beautiful painting and carvings, and should be preserved.

WALL PAINTINGS

A.C. Edwards

In the Middle Ages, the walls of most churches were covered with paintings on plaster; today, only a small part of this heritage survives. At the Reformation they were whitewashed over; later, especially in Victorian times, many of them were completely destroyed when "restorers", unaware of these hidden treasures, and ignorant of the meaning and purpose of those already exposed, stripped the plaster from the walls. Within the past century or so, a number of paintings have been uncovered and, in recent years at least, skilfully treated. Even now, however, examples very occasionally occur of deliberate destruction of newly-found paintings.

In Essex, as in some other south-eastern counties, the survival rate is relatively high. There are around 50 Essex churches with paintings from medieval or Tudor times. About a dozen churches have 17th century examples, mainly of inscriptions in black letter. *Theydon Mount*, for instance, has a Creed and a Lord's Prayer of 1611-14. *Fairstead* has an interesting prayer for James I and the Royal Family. Many of the medieval paintings are fragmentary and scarcely discernable; some are of the highest artistic quality, comparable with any in the land. However, those who have had the pleasure of listening, spellbound, to Clive Rouse will know that aesthetic merit was scarcely in the minds of medieval painters. They were *teachers*: their paintings were visual aids for the religious education of illiterate worshippers; every look, every gesture in the figures they depicted was charged with meaning and dire warning. They would have little to learn from their modern counterpart, the strip cartoonist, certainly nothing of moral significance. They often depicted the most awful prospect for Christians—The Doom, or Last Judgment—above the chancel arch, where none could fail to see it and tremble. At *Woodham Ferrers*, Christ the Judge is seated on a rainbow, with angels on His right and souls below. Hell's mouth is in the lower right corner, and a dread message in black letter reads, *Surgite incriminati ad judicium dei*—"let the guilty rise before the judgment of God."

Pre-eminent among Essex paintings are those at *Copford* church, a building of considerable architectural interest standing in a delightful setting. Its surviving paintings were executed about 1140-50 when the church was built. The set piece covers the whole of the apse. It was rediscovered in 1871 and heavily restored in the following year. Saints and archangels fill the lowest tier. Above them are the buildings of New Jerusalem and angels supporting a circular rainbow; within the rainbow, dominating the scene, is the figure of Christ in Majesty. In the rest of the church are other paintings, including the signs of the Zodiac on the soffit of the arch leading to the apse. On the north side of the nave, within a semi-circle and fortunately unrestored, is the Raising of Jairus's Daughter. Jairus, at the entrance to his house, wears a black 'Jew's hat'; his features are markedly Semitic; his eyes are full of anxiety; his whole pose is one of entreaty. The head of Christ is inclined towards him; His expression is infinitely compassionate. It is a moving picture, beautifully articulated.

In an arched recess behind the altar of *Great Canfield* church is a painting of the Virgin and Child, a painting of the highest quality, full of tenderness. Sir Nikolaus Pevsner dates it c.1250 on the analogy of the Matthew Paris manuscripts. It is executed in red, with some yellow for the gold of the throne and the hair and haloes of the subjects. Below is a large white formy consecration cross on red, within white and yellow circles.

The paintings in *Fairstead* church, executed in red and yellow ochres and black and white, are mostly of the second half of the thirteenth century and the first half of the fourteenth. They were discovered about 1890, but it was not until the 1930s that they were fully examined by the late Professor E.W. Tristram, who treated all those which were decipherable. They are not of high artistic quality, but they are lively enough to have served their purpose well. Those over the chancel arch depict the Passion. Perhaps the best illustrates the Betrayal. In the centre is the Kiss of Judas. To the right is a Roman soldier in 13th century armour; with one hand he grasps the wrist of Christ, while the other holds a lantern aloft. To the left, St Peter is shown cutting off the ear of Malchus, servant to Caiaphas; the painter was determined that the incident should not be missed—the sword and the ear are both large.

Among its wide range of fittings, *Little Easton* church has interesting paintings, discovered c.1883 and restored by Professor Tristram in 1934. The fifteenth century series of eight Passion subjects is indistinct in parts and of moderate artistic merit. The large figure of an apostle or evangelist, painted c.1195 has suffered some defacement and fading, but enough remains to show that it was of the finest quality. Originally it was underpainted in black (which now shows in places, notably the features) and then the red and yellow ochres were applied. The painting is full of declamatory vigour; the book, clasped in the left hand, is closed; the prophet or apostle is clearly not short of words, and probably stern ones at that. It is suggested that he may be the only survivor of a series of the Twelve Apostles, possibly as part of a *Coelum* or Paradise.

75. *Copford. Christ in Majesty.*

75

76b. *Great Canfield. Virgin and Child, c. 1250.*

76a. *Little Easton. An Apostle or Evangelist, c. 1175.*

St Christopher was one of the most popular subjects with medieval painters. He was the patron saint of travellers and , as Clive Rouse points out, his story teaches salvation through service. In most churches his figure was painted on the wall facing the main entrance, and this was usually the south door; thus it greeted the traveller or the regular worshipper as he entered the church. The early fifteenth century St Christopher at *Little Baddow* was discovered in 1922 by the rector, Canon Jesse Berridge. He knew from documentary evidence that a St Christopher had been covered over; and so, when craftsmen were working on the north wall, he ordered that any trace of colour was to be reported immediately. When this happened, he and two of his sons carefully removed the covering plaster with old kitchen knives. An even finer and slightly older St Christopher was discovered at *Lambourne* in 1951; part of the painting was destroyed by eighteenth century alterations, but the saint's head and the figure of the Christ Child have survived. There is a large and complete example of c.1510 at *Layer Marney,* while fragmentary remains survive at *Fingringhoe* and *Orsett.*

Two other churches are well worth visiting, even though their paintings are faded and fragmentary. They are *Bradwell-juxta-Coggeshall* and *Hadleigh.* The early 14th century paintings at Bradwell are of specially high quality whilst at Hadleigh the painting of Thomas-à-Becket c.1171 is of considerable interest. At *Tilbury-juxta-Clare* is a late 15th century painting of a timber-framed house.

Stories of lost paintings make sad reading, but it is of some consolation if an adequate record has been preserved. In 1876, when the historian, G.C. Coulton, was a boy at Felsted School, he made two sketches of a painting discovered in *Felsted* church and then foolishly destroyed. They show Avarice, doubtless one of a series on the Seven Deadly Sins. It is personified by a miser counting his gold and egged on by two hairy demons. His four-legged table rests on the thick stem of a vine, with its roots in the open jaws of Hell. Two other demons are busily sawing at the stem with a cross-cut saw. The vicar and restorer of the church in 1876, left the original painting on view for a time and "then broke it away, as it was considered too lurid for the eyes of worshippers in mid-Victorian times." But how did it appear to 14th century worshippers? One must assume that humour was used with the intention of making the serious message stick.

A document in the Petre archives is headed 'Lyght Kyne', and gives a glimpse of the interior of *Ingatestone* church at the eve of the Reformation. It is a list of church cows rented to villagers, the income going to the upkeep of lights before specified 'images' and various fittings. The list begins with 'The Image of saynt Edmonde,' the patron saint of the church. Other images include St Nicholas, the Trinity, St John the Baptist, Our Lady of Grace, St Michael and St Christopher. As a wallpainting of St Christopher was discovered in 1866 on the north wall of the nave and then replastered, it is reasonable to assume that some of the 'images' were paintings, not three-dimensional figures. A somewhat similar list of church goods at *Little Waltham,* c.1410-20, mentions lights before figures of St Peter, St James, St Andrew, St Nicholas, St Margaret, St Anne and the Blessed Virgin Mary. These, too, could have been paintings.

GRAFFITI

Christopher Starr

"Dum sumus in mundo, vivamus corde jocundo"—a short life and a merry one—so runs a graffito on the wall of *Little Dunmow* church, probably inscribed by a monk with the point of his stylus five hundred years ago. From the early Middle Ages, graffiti—scribbled drawings or inscriptions—have been scratched on the stonework of Essex churches and the hundreds of surviving but generally neglected examples provide a revealing glimpse of our forbears.

The quality and spontaneity of graffiti varies greatly, most of them appear to have been swiftly and lightly scratched though some were deeply cut, occasionally with great skill and the use of a chisel. Particular care was often lavished on inscriptions, two examples of which (from *Terling* and *Little Dunmow*) are illustrated. What impelled these medieval wall scribblers to register their feelings cannot always be determined but it should be remembered that the majority of early inscriptions must be attributed to the clergy since nearly everyone else was illiterate. "Secular" inscriptions, where they do exist, tend to be no more than the name or initials of the writer.

Graffiti are generally to be found inside rather than outside churches, rarely above eye-level and usually scratched on stonework. There are exceptions, they can, for example, be seen on the external brickwork at *Ingrave* and on the wooden pews at *Fobbing*. Graffiti are most likely to be found on columns, doorways, tower arches, window sills and rood loft stairs.

Comparatively little research has been done on Essex graffiti and it is sometimes difficult to distinguish them from other marks and signs which are to be found in churches. There are an enormous number of masons' marks which may seem to be simple graffiti but are in fact the "signatures" of individual masons or lodges. An excellent series of such marks is to be seen on the tower doorway at *Rawreth* and there are others at *Asheldham, Fordham, Little Totham, Pitsea, Paglesham, Runwell Rochford* and *Dedham*. Often confused with graffiti are sun dials scratched on the south-facing walls of churches—these are generally incised circles with lines 15 degrees apart radiating from a central hole once containing a peg or pin—as at *Little Burstead, Great Burstead, Burnham-on-Crouch, Elmstead, Great Wakering, Ashingdon* and *Great Bentley*. Consecration crosses—such as the pair at *Southminster*, may also be mistaken for graffiti.

Although a large number of graffiti survive, probably many more have disappeared; some as a result of nineteenth century restorations when stonework was vigorously scraped clean and others buried under successive layers of whitewash. A few, like those at *Alphamstone*, are gradually disappearing as damp walls crumble to dust. A serious problem with graffiti is of course, in deciding whether they are genuine survivals or contemporary examples. There is no easy solution to this difficulty but on balance, an inscription's origins are more easily determined than those of a drawing.

One of the oldest known graffiti in Essex is at *Belchamp Walter* where there is a stone bearing the date 1217 in Roman numerals—though this probably came from an earlier building. The dates 1301 and 1340 are to be found on inscriptions at *Steeple Bumpstead* and *Finchingfield* respectively. Names, sometimes with accompanying dates, are often found—*Rickling, Sible Hedingham, Little Sampford*, and *Toppesfield*. A particularly interesting example of c.1480 is at *Rayleigh*. Early clergymen, particularly in the sixteenth century, recorded their names on the walls of their churches and several may be seen at *Belchamp Walter, Alphamstone* and *Stanford-le-Hope*. At *Hatfield Peverel* there is a brief reference to Edmund Alleyne dated 1597, he was patron of the church at the time.

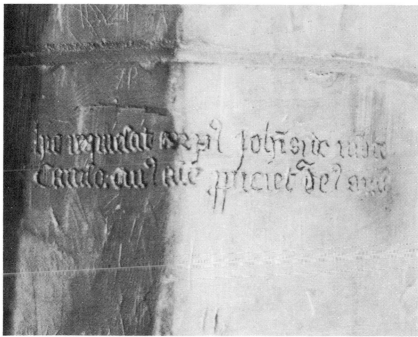

79a. *Little Dunmow. Memorial inscription.*

79b. *Elmstead. Scratch dial.*

79c. *Wethersfield. Damaged corbel improved by a graffito.*

Fig. 9. *Willingale Spain. Crossbows.*

Fig. 8. *Terling. Shield of arms and inscription.*

80

In the days before parish registers, references to burials were occasionally scratched on church walls, *Chrishall* and *Little Dunmow* having examples, whilst there is a reference to a marriage which took place in 1358 at *Steeple Bumpstead*. In pre-Reformation England marriages were solemnised in the church porch rather than at the altar and in recognition of their vows the couple would scratch a cross on the wall—many such crosses being visible today. A number of poignant messages which even now convey the writer's anguish can be read on church walls such as "God help me" at *Steeple Bumpstead*, and, "Marye Helpe" at *Hatfield Broad Oak*. Other inscriptions, the lines of doggerel at *Ridgewell*, a lover's motto at *Rickling* and the exquisite "Amor vincit omnia" at *Clavering* convey a different message. Staves of music can be found at *Steeple Bumpstead* and *Rayleigh* and a harp at *Kelvedon*.

Many of the graffiti drawings have an heraldic connection—shields of arms occur in at least twenty churches, notably at *Canewdon, Lindsell, Great Chesterford, Roydon, Elsenham, Writtle, Downham, West Thurrock, Witham* and *White Notley*. At least three churches, *Thaxted, Sible Hedingham* and *Stebbing* have the heraldic knot of the Bourchier family scratched on their walls. Weapons too are occasionally seen, a longbow and quiver at *Kelvedon*, crossbows at *Little Totham* and *Willingale Spain*, arrows at *White Notley*.

Christian symbolism is common—though a Crucifix is rarely depicted, perhaps uniquely at *Ridgewell*. Crosses in many forms can be seen in dozens of churches including *Boreham, Aveley, Great Henny* and *Hadleigh*, chalices at *Great Chesterford* and *Chrishall;* Alpha and Omega at *Alphamstone* and a Sacred Heart at *Elsenham*. At *Copford* is an example of ecclesiastical heraldry—a shield with the symbol of the Holy Trinity. Hints of ancient magic crop up at *Downham, Elsenham* and *South Weald* where there are pentacles and at *Little Waltham* and *Sible Hedingham* with Solomon's Knots.

The human form is variously portrayed—faces at *Elsenham* and *Sible Hedingham*, bishops at *Finchingfield, Willingale Spain* and *White Notley*, a hooded figure at *Terling*, and a priest at *Lindsell*. Curiously, there does not seem to be a single medieval representation of a woman in an Essex church in the form of a graffito.

Birds occur at *Lindsell* and *Sible Hedingham*, fish at *Great Yeldham*, a snake and a dog at *Steeple Bumpstead*, a horse at *Alphamstone* and antlers at *Wormingford*. Flowers are rarer, but have been drawn at *Thaxted* and *Belchamp Walter*, at *Wethersfield* a damaged corbel has been redesigned as a giant daisy.

As has been said, the study of medieval graffiti is in its infancy and there is ample scope for further research. Rubbings of graffiti can easily be made using a 3H pencil on good quality thin paper. The rubbings are generally small enough to be mounted on A4 paper and stored in loose-leaf binders. It is comparatively easy to build a collection on a particular theme, for example, one could begin with ships using graffiti at *Rainham, Kelvedon, Willingale Spain, Little Waltham* and *Chadwell St Mary*.

BELLS

Peter Came

The oldest man-made sound to be heard across the Essex countryside is that from the church bell and for centuries this unique sound has been made to summon the living, to mourn the dead and to declare national days of rejoicing.

Rings, wrongly called peals, of bells, diatonically tuned, contain 4,5,6,8,10 or 12 bells, each bell weighing anything from a few hundredweight to as many tons. In the old geographical county of Essex there are about 1175 bells, contained in 176 rings of from 5 to 12 bells, and there are at least another 510 bells contained in towers with between one and four bells. About 160 of all these bells are of Pre-Reformation date. Historically bells form an important body of tangible and valuable evidence concerning a unique form of metal working through many centuries. Moreover, since bells are composed of bronze, approximately 77 per cent copper and 23 per cent tin, they are also of value to the dishonest scrap dealer who can market such metal for a quick monetary return. It is unfortunate that the four bells, three of seventeenth and one of eighteenth century date, disappeared in this way from *East Horndon* in 1969.

Bells made of bronze for hanging in church towers were being cast in England in the seventh century, but the earliest evidence of casting in this county comes from *Hadstock*. A furnace for casting bronze bells, perhaps of tenth century date, together with the nearby holes that contained the bell moulds, was found within the seventh century walls of Hadstock church during the extensive archaeological investigations carried out in 1974.

There are few bells in existence in England dating from before 1200. Perhaps the earliest bells in Essex are the uninscribed pair hanging in *Little Braxted* belfry: they embody all the features common to "early" bells. They are of small diameter, 18 and 18½ inches, they are long waisted and almost straight-sided with metal of uniform thickness except on the outside of the sound bow. Apply Elphick's chronology, based on the morphology of "early" bells, then the *Little Braxted* pair would fit a date of c.1230.

Most early bellfounders were olarii, makers of metal pots, and the potters' tradition determined that the sound bow of "early" bells should be thickened on the outside like the rim of a pot. It is, therefore, no coincidence that the surname "Potter" is found amongst bellfounders. Walter le Potter and Adam le Potter were London bellfounders of the second half of the thirteenth century and Thomas Potter, "Brasyer" of Norwich, cast a bell, the present tenor, for *Gosfield* in the early fifteenth century. Robert Rider (fl. 1357-86), who cast the third at *Ridgewell,* also carried on the trade of potter.

Many early bells like those at Little Braxted were probably moulded on a horizontal "lathe", as illustrated in the Richard Tunnoc bellfounder's window of c.1330 in York Minster; but such a "lathe" produced technical problems which limited the diameter of the bells. It was not easy to mould a core of a large modern shaped bell in clay horizontally. These technical difficulties were overcome during the thirteenth century, however, when bells were being moulded and modelled in an upright position. This enabled the founders to alter the height and diameter to obtain the correct note. It also enabled them to change the whole shape of the bell so that on the outside the waist became concave and gradually thickened towards the convex shaped sound bow (Fig. 10).

With the solving of many technical problems during the thirteenth century it became normal practice to vary the weight and diameter of the bells within a ring so that the treble, the smallest bell, gave forth the highest note and the tenor, the largest bell, the lowest note. Hitherto the different notes had been obtained by casting all

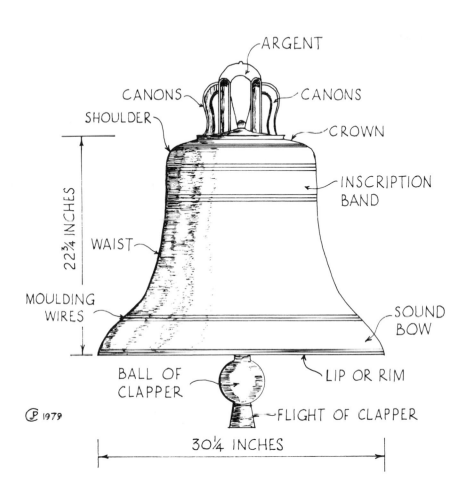

ARGENT

CANONS

CANONS

SHOULDER

CROWN

INSCRIPTION BAND

22¾ INCHES

WAIST

MOULDING WIRES

SOUND BOW

BALL OF CLAPPER

LIP OR RIM

℗ 1979

FLIGHT OF CLAPPER

30¼ INCHES

Fig.10. *The parts of a bell. Based on a bell in Heybridge church by John Danyell c.1450.*

the bells of a ring to approximately the same diameter, but altering the thickness of the metal.

All bells cast before the mid-nineteenth century had "handles." The large loop, the argent, was "buttressed" in six places by smaller loops called canons (Fig. 10). The argent was the largest and strongest loop as it had to withstand the downward thrust of at least four times the weight of the bell when it was being swung full circle. This complicated structure had to be modelled separately as the bell had to be "strapped" to an elm headstock, with gudgeons at each end, so that it could swing freely and be allowed to fully vibrate when struck with a clapper (Fig. 16).

Not all medieval bells necessarily bear the maker's name, but there are other tell tales. Bells are frequently ornamented not only with beautiful lettering but also with "stops," trade marks, shields and other decorations. England's earliest inscribed bell, dating from between 1207 and 1219 at Caversfield, Oxon, has lettering that is Roman in form, but from the fourteenth century onwards two varieties of letter were used: Gothic capitals and black letter "small." Black letter "smalls" are frequently used with initial Gothic capitals; this style is known as mixed Gothic. During the fourteenth century the use of capital letters throughout is universal and no black letter type is found before c.1400. The use of Gothic capitals is well seen on the third bell at *Fairstead* which was cast by Peter de Weston (fl.1328-47). Mixed Gothic lettering, as well as other decoration, occurs on the four Pre-Reformation bells at *Margaretting*. All four bells are by different London founders. The third, the oldest, is by Robert Burford (fl.1392-1418); the tenor by John Walgrave (fl.1418-40); the second by William Culverden (fl.1506-22); and the treble by Thomas Lawrence (fl.1523-38). In addition to its circular "stops" the treble has four figures intended either for the Good Shepherd or St John the Baptist with a lamb (Fig. 11).

'Trade marks' were also introduced and William Culverden's is the most elaborate of them all with a subtle rebus device (Fig.12). The letters "fown" of the word "founder" occur on the bell; culver is an old English word for pigeon, the bird represented on his shield. Combine the culver with the W and the de and we thus obtain W. Culverden.

Henry Jordan's (fl.1442-70) bells were usually inscribed with a dedication to a saint together with shields and a medallion. The heraldic shield (Fig.13) shows cross keys and a dolphin naiant which are the arms of the Fishmongers' Company to which he belonged; the wheatsheaf was the cognisance of the family of Harleton from which he was descended; while the bell and the laver pot are obvious references to Jordan's trade. The other shield (Fig.14) is of the merchant mark type and is known as the "banner" shield. Usually accompanying the shields is a beautiful medallion with the words, "ihu mercy ladi help," between the arms of the cross (Fig.7). At *Woodham Walter* the second bell by Jordan has neither inscription nor "cross keys" shield, but has been identified as a bell of that founder by the "banner" shield and "ihu mercy" medallion.

In the late sixteenth and early seventeenth centuries Gothic gradually gave way to Roman lettering and it became usual for the founder to declare his name on bells he cast. It was in the seventeenth century that Essex was to have its own most famous bellfounder, Miles Graye of Colchester. He did not originate the foundry however. Richard Bowler was casting in Colchester between 1587 and 1604. He used ornamental Gothic on *Fairstead* tenor in 1601 and Roman lettering on *Ridgewell* treble in 1600, but the second bell in that tower is inscribed "JESUS BE OUR SPEDE" in Gothic and "RICARDUS BOWLER ME? FECIT 1901 (1601)" in Roman lettering.

Miles Graye I, born c.1575, was apprenticed to Bowler and married his domestic servant. He died in 1649 "crazed with age and weak in body." His son, Miles, he cut off with a shilling and no more is heard of him after his father's death; but a subsequent Miles Graye III, whose bells are common between 1650 and 1686, must have been a grandson. Miles Graye I was responsible for the beautiful tenor at Lavenham just across the Essex border in Suffolk. Miles Graye III appears to have been responsible for the splendid toned "maiden" five of 1634 in the round tower at

Fig.11. *Margaretting. Figure from treble bell c.1530.*

Fig.12. *Takeley. Rebus trade mark of William Culverden c. 1515.*

85

Fig.13. *Pitsea. Shield from bell by Henry Jordan c.1455.*

Fig.14. *Banner shield and medallion from bell by Henry Jordan.*

MILES 🪆 GR AYE 🪆 MADE 🪆
ME 🪆 1622

Fig.15. *St James', Colchester. Inscription from bell by Miles Graye I.*

Great Leighs and the four put up in *Purleigh* in 1636. Nearly all the Miles Graye family bells with exceptions, bear the briefest of inscription: "Miles Graye made me," the date and, in 1622 only, some ornamental square 'stops' were introduced (Fig.15). The early lettering from 1600 to 1612 has strokes of uniform thickness and rough execution. In 1612 this lettering takes on a bold Roman form and between 1632 and 1642 the usual formula of the Graye inscription is converted into Latin: MILONEM GRAYE ME FECIT. There are still about 175 Graye family bells extant in Essex. Miles Graye III died at Colchester in 1686 and Henry Pleasant appears to have filled the vacuum caused by Graye's death. Pleasant, who started a foundry at Sudbury, Suffolk, in 1691, is famous for his punning rhymes. At *Maldon, All Saints* (recast in 1922), the first four of the six bells were inscribed in large plain type thus:

Treble	WHEN THREE THIS STEEPLE LONG DID HOLD
2	THEY WERE THREE EMBLEMS OF A SCOLD
3	NO MVSICK THEN BUT NOW SHALL SEE
4	WHAT PLEASANT MVSICK SIX WILL BE

About 20 of Pleasant's bells remain in Essex including the single bell in *Little Tey* church inscribed "HENRY PLEASANT DID ME RUNN ANNO 1701".

Thomas Gardiner then started a rival foundry in Sudbury which flourished from 1709 to 1760. Not all his bells were cast at Sudbury. He "itinerated" in 1739 and cast a bell for *Great Chesterford* at Ingatestone. There are still well over 50 of Gardiner's bells in Essex.

From the late eighteenth century onwards Essex again came under the influence of the London foundries. Thomas Mears (Whitechapel Foundry) cast a new eight for *Writtle* in 1811. His successors recast the tenor, sixth and second in 1916; recast the fifth after an accident in 1952; and in 1979 the Whitechapel Foundry rehung these bells on roller bearings. John Warner & Sons of Cripplegate cast a new ring of six for *Widford* in 1862; a new octave for *Galleywood* in 1873; a new six for *Great Totham* in 1878; and a new twelve (tenor 34½ cwt.) for *Chelmsford pro-Cathedral* in 1913.

The Croydon clock firm of Gillett & Johnston also cast bells for Essex churches. Their bells are highly individualistic and very resonant in tone, a result of their having put into practice the tuning theories of Canon Simpson (1828-1900) who was writing at the end of the nineteenth century. This firm recast the third, fourth and fifth of the old octave at *Thaxted* in 1948-49.

John Taylor & Co. of Loughborough have done some very good work in Essex during the twentieth century and their most worthy contribution to the bell founders' art is the beautifully toned, mellow eight at *Great Baddow* cast in 1924 and their most recent ring is the recast ten at *West Ham* in 1979.

From time to time it has become necessary to recast bells for many reasons, such as faulty castings and accidents caused by the bell falling out of its mountings or its path being fouled by a clock hammer or even by clocking - tying a rope to the flight of the clapper and the clapper pulled against the side of the bell. Some bells, however, crack from the crown. This is because the cast in crown staple of iron, to which the clapper is attached, rusts and expands and in doing so cracks the crown of the bell. Unfortunately, the fourth bell at *Boreham*, cast by Thomas Lester (Whitechapel Foundry) in 1746, has such a hair crack in the crown and may have to be recast.

Churchwardens' accounts abound in instances of recasting. John Tonne recast the tenor at *Great Hallingbury* in 1542. He also cast three other bells and one of these is the present third. The term "new running the bells" is often applied where bells were recast, such is the case at *Danbury* where Thomas Gardiner recast two earlier bells in 1759.

Sometimes casting or recasting was carried out on site. In the 1640's an unknown founder came to the village of *Writtle* and cast a new treble. It is likely that the casting was done within the church (cf. Hadstock) as Thomas Manning was paid 16s "for taking up the fournace and makinge clene the Church."

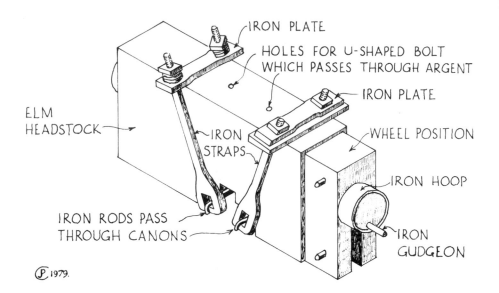

IRON PLATE

HOLES FOR U-SHAPED BOLT
WHICH PASSES THROUGH ARGENT

IRON PLATE

ELM
HEADSTOCK

WHEEL POSITION

IRON
STRAPS

IRON HOOP

IRON RODS PASS
THROUGH CANONS

IRON
GUDGEON

P. 1979.

Fig.16. *The argent and canons of a bell are "strapped" to an elm headstock. This sixteenth century example supports the John Danyell bell at Heybridge.*

These days there are restrictions on what can be done to church bells. The Council for Places of Worship has formal agreements with the two remaining bellfounders which require that no bells cast prior to 1600 are recast and in some circumstances no bells dating from before 1750 can be recast either. In addition where pre-seventeenth century bells are good examples of their kind the bellfounders are not allowed to remove the canons. At *Purleigh* the canons were preserved on the four Miles Graye bells when the ring was rehung in 1973. On the other hand permission is given to recast pre-1750 bells if they are poor examples of their type. At *Danbury,* for example, two Miles Graye bells were of such poor tonal quality, they had been badly knocked about and the canons were missing, that recasting was allowed provided the original inscriptions were preserved in facsimile on the new bells cast in 1967. Indeed, if a post-1750 bell is recast then its inscription too must be reproduced in facsimile on the new bell.

Added to these precautions a Faculty has to be sought from the Diocesan authorities and the Diocesan Advisory Committee inspects all plans and is guided by advice from experts in the field of bells and bell frames before any work can be carried out. Advice can also be sought from the Central Council of Church Bellringers which has a Towers and Belfries advisory committee.

Lastly, where churches have become disused a home is found for the bells no longer needed. Recently the bell from the bombed church of *St Stephen's, Upton Park,* has made a sixth bell for the ring at *Ingrave.*

ORGANS

Gillian Ward Russell and Anthony Russell

It cannot be said that Essex offers to the connoisseur of church organs many enormous monsters, indeed, we are only going to mention two large organs in the county, one at *Chelmsford Cathedral* and the other at *Saffron Walden* parish church. However, to the true lover of the instrument, size is not of prime importance. Quality and variety of tone are of greater interest and in these aspects of the instrument, Essex can give to the discerning searcher an infinite variety of pleasure.

Whilst it is not possible even to mention every instrument of interest in this short article, it is our wish to encourage the reader to look at the organs in our churches—not just the cases, but the maker, and the type of stops to be found on the instrument. Even better, if interest is aroused, to try to hear the instrument played; for not only are they played at services but there are recitals and flower festivals where instruments are demonstrated even in the smallest churches.

In Essex there are many small church organs whose makers' names have disappeared from the instrument, but seem to have been well made and maintained. Such an organ can be found at *Steeple*: although small, it fills the church with sound and it has only one manual, four stops and three composition pedals. A brass plate states "Erected by Voluntary Contributions October 6:1859" but the organ was not made for this church. It was intended for *St Mary's, Burnham*, being taken to Steeple later—as the plate on the side of the organ states. Another small organ of note is at *Lamarsh*. This is a fine example of the work of G.P. England and has been kept not only in excellent—but in its original condition. The church itself is well worth a visit, but we believe the organ to be a treasure without equal, although it has only three stops—Dulciana, Stopt Diapason, Principal—and is still hand-pumped. This instrument remains in weekly use, and recitals and broadcasts have been made on it. An interesting feature is that the keyboard folds away into the instrument.

At *Little Bardfield* there is a newly-restored small organ built by the well-known, and much respected organ builder Renatus Harris who died in 1724. It has an attractive case probably designed by Harris himself and built by G.Gibbon. The organ is quite small but has a fine strong tone (although it was much out of tune when we played it); and with eleven stops (which include a Cornet, Sequaltera and Trumpet) it can give in variety and quality a sound equal to many larger instruments, the only additions to the original instrument appear to be an electric blower and a few pedal pipes.

There are several good examples of the work of Holditch in the county. Three well-preserved instruments can be seen at *Fingringhoe, Birch* and *St Mary's, Ilford*. An interesting feature of Holditch's instruments is the inclusion of the stop invented by him (and found on very few instruments) the Diaocton. The *Fingringhoe* organ having the characteristic narrow pedals, ornately painted show pipes (the bottom octave of the Open Diapason painted in grey and gold). The Birch organ built in 1844, was carefully restored by Mander in 1965, and the cost of the work met by a couple in thanks for their diamond wedding.

At *St Michael's, Braintree*, the organ contains examples of work by two builders: the Great Organ is by Holditch (c.1860); the Swell Organ was added in 1886 by August Gern, foreman of the great French romantic organ builder Cavaillé-Coll. The whole organ was overhauled by Mander in 1948 and he carried out further work on it in 1975.

Father Willis built many fine organs, notably at Alexandra Palace; and a few examples of his work may be seen in Essex. The organ at *St Andrew's, Halstead,* was built about 1886 and was enlarged by Willis Jr. in 1919. This instrument can still give a good account of itself, and is an excellent instrument on which to perform music of the late nineteenth and early twentieth centuries. Noted as a builder of large organs,

90a. *Birch. Holditch organ.*

90b. *Lamarsh. Fold-away manual on G.P. England organ.*

90

Father Willis was also at home with small ones, as the Model Organ at *Foxearth* shows.

An organ with an interesting and unusual history can be seen at *St Nicholas' Church, Harwich*. Built in 1822 by Flight and Robson of London, it was later bought second-hand for this church, but en route for Harwich the barge carrying it sank in the Thames during a storm. This might have been the end of the organ, but in fact, it was later salvaged and it eventually arrived at its present position, in the West Gallery at St Nicholas'. Apart from its strange history, it has a pleasing appearance and a fairly unusual stop, a Mounted Cornet. It was in need of an overhaul when we played it, but even so, it produced a fine tone.

There are several examples of the work of Hill in the county—the small organ at *Gosfield* being particularly interesting. Although small, this instrument has a useful range of stops, and is capable of filling the small church with sound. Some alterations have been made to the original instrument, but these have been tastefully carried out and both the sound and appearance must be now very much as they would have been originally.

The fine instrument at *Coggeshall*, built by Bishop in 1839 was partially destroyed during the last war. The rebuilding was carried out by Mander, who, while incorporating many of the old pipes, included some additions. The pipework is situated at the west end of the church, while the console is in the Lady chapel near the choir, having the advantage (once the inevitable delay has been accounted for) of enabling the organist to direct the choir. The instrument has only two manuals but a large number of stops; it has the resources to carry out fully its function in services and for the many recitals and concerts held in the church.

The organ at *Saffron Walden* is of considerable interest. Originally an instrument suitable for the size of the church, but containing little of outstanding interest, the organ was rebuilt and enlarged by Hill, Norman and Beard 1971-1972, incorporating earlier pipework: Vincent (1824), T.C. Lewis (1858) and Norman and Beard (1911). It is now situated on the screen with what is in reality a four manual instrument based on three manuals. The Trompeta Real is of particular interest and can be seen pointing into the church from the south chapel.

The development of the *Cathedral* organ follows the development of the cathedral itself, it gradually grew larger as the building became more important in the county. When the nave collapsed in 1800 the old organ was enlarged by Hugh Russell. Since then, the work of enlarging and extending the organ by various builders has gone on until the present instrument now has four manuals. Like the organs in so many English churches its position unfortunately does not allow the sound to do it full justice and the listener needs to choose his seat carefully at a recital if he is to hear the organ at its best.

A few years after the last war, an interest in recreating the sound of the Baroque organ developed; the characteristics of this type of organ being: a bright, light and clear sound as opposed to the thick warm sound of the Romantic organ. Such an instrument being most suitable for playing the music of the Baroque period upon, and an example of such an organ can be seen at *St Mary's, Woodford*. This instrument, built by Grant, Degens and Bradbeer in 1972, fits well into the modern building and enhances the appearance of the church. To the organist it presents some problems as it is quite impossible to judge the balance of sound from the console, this is of course, true of many other organs.

We hope that this short review of some Essex organs will help visitors to look at, listen to and perhaps even play many of the organs we have had to leave out. It would be pleasant to think that future writers of church guides would add a paragraph about their organ and its history. Many of us, to whom a visit to a town or village is highlighted by a glance around the church, would like to know a little information concerning the instrument which is of so much importance in the worship of today.

REDUNDANT CHURCHES
IN THE DIOCESE

William Grosvenor

The Nature and Extent of the problem

In 1960 the Bridges Report estimated that some 790 Church of England churches would become redundant in the period up to 1980. In accordance with the recommendations of that report a statutory procedure was established for dealing with redundant churches by the Pastoral Measure of 1968. Under the terms of this legislation the future of any church declared to be pastorally redundant must lie between preservation, appropriation to an alternative use or demolition. Up to 31 March 1979 758 churches were declared redundant under the Pastoral Measure. In July 1979 figures released by the Church Commissioners showed that approximately 48% of redundant churches were being appropriated to an alternative use, 22% preserved and 30% demolished. In the Diocese of Chelmsford, comprising the modern administrative county of Essex and the five East London Boroughs of Newham, Redbridge, Waltham Forest, Barking and Havering all historically part of Essex, the future of some 42 redundant churches, some of long standing, has been decided under the terms of the Measure. Twenty-five of them have been appropriated to an alternative use, 3 preserved by the Redundant Churches Fund and 12 demolished, whilst at the time of writing the future of two others remains to be settled.

Expressed simply, the problem facing the Church of England is the conflict between its modern pastoral needs and its historic and architectural legacy. Many churches are either too large or in the wrong places and expensive to maintain, yet of nearly 18,000 parish churches some 11,500 are buildings listed as being of special historic or architectural interest. It is in this context that the problem of redundancy must be viewed.

It is largely a modern problem. The changing face of our inner city areas, their declining population, together with the redevelopment potential of valuable sites, have all led to the frequent replacement of large old churches with smaller more convenient ones. The demolition of *Leyton, All Saints* and *Plaistow, St Mary* is illustrative of the changing pastoral requirements of such areas. In the countryside the shift of population and changing farming methods have also required pastoral reorganisation, although less so in Essex than in the neighbouring East Anglian counties. Declining congregations find the maintenance of medieval buildings too much of a burden to bear, whilst a reduction in the number of available clergy has meant less time to organise effective appeals. Many rural churches are in isolated positions like the remote *Tolleshunt Knights,* the delightful *Chickney, St Mary* and the rare (in Essex) 18th century church of *St Peter and St Paul, Shellow Bowells.* The historic location of many parish churches adjacent to the Manor House often means they are far from the villages they serve, as at *West Bergholt.* Where access is difficult or where there is an alternative place of worship within the village itself, the remote parish church becomes progressively less used and thus eventually falls redundant. *East Horndon, Latchingdon, St Michael* and *Langdon Hills, St Mary and All Saints* are all typical examples in this respect.

The procedure of Redundancy

The initiative for declaring a church formally redundant may come from the Diocesan Pastoral Committee or from within the parish itself. The Pastoral Committee must then ascertain the views of the Council for Places of Worship and obtain information about the historic and architectural qualities of the building. The Pastoral Committee must also find out the views of all "interested parties", defined as the

93a. *Chickney.*

93b. *West Bergholt.*

incumbent, the patron of the benefice, the Parochial Church Council, the Archdeacon, the Rural Dean and the local planning authority. When the views of the Council for Places of Worship and the interested parties are known, the Diocesan Pastoral Committee will decide whether to proceed further. If they decide to do so and the Bishop approves, the proposals are forwarded to the Church Commissioners to prepare a draft Pastoral Scheme to make the church redundant. At this stage, the Advisory Board for Redundant Churches may be consulted. Copies of the draft Pastoral Scheme are served on the interested parties and on the Advisory Board. A notice is published in local and national newspapers and posted on the church door giving brief details of the proposals and allowing 28 days for objections to be lodged . If the Commissioners are satisfied that the church is no longer required as a parish church or chapel of ease the draft Scheme is submitted to the Bishop for his consent. When he has given his consent the Scheme is sealed and submitted for confirmation by Her Majesty in Council, after allowing a final period of 28 days for appeal to the Privy Council. The Scheme normally comes into effect on the date of publication of the Notice of Confirmation.

Upon the taking effect of a Declaration of Redundancy the liability of the Parochial Church Council to repair and maintain the church ceases and the building vests in the Diocesan Board of Finance. The Church Commissioners consult the Advisory Board as to the merits of preservation whilst the Diocesan Redundant Churches Uses Committee will make every endeavour to find a suitable alternative use. If this is successful then a Redundancy Scheme will be prepared authorising the appropriation to the approved new use. If the church merits preservation in the national interest the Commissioners may prepare a Scheme providing for its vesting in the Redundant Churches Fund. If the search is unsuccessful and the building does not merit preservation then a Scheme will be prepared providing for its demolition. The Commissioners are required to prepare a Redundancy Scheme after a period of at least one year and not more than three years after the Pastoral Scheme has come into effect. A copy of the draft Scheme is served on the Diocesan Board of Finance, the local planning authority, the Advisory Board and the Redundant Churches Fund if the draft Scheme provides for vesting the building in that body. A notice is placed in the local press allowing 28 days for objections. If the Commissioners decide to proceed they will seal a copy of the draft Scheme and submit it for confirmation to Her Majesty in Council. During this waiting period the Redundant Churches Fund may contribute to the cost of any necessary repairs particularly with regard to those churches which are likely to be subsequently vested in it as in the case of *East Horndon*. A long waiting period, however, can expose an already vunerable building to yet more decay and vandalism as happened with *Colchester Holy Trinity*.

Preservation

The Redundant Churches Fund is a body set up under Part III of the Pastoral Measure 1968 to preserve in the interests of the nation and the Church of England churches or parts of churches of historic or architectural interest vested in it. The Fund is financed jointly by grants from the Church Commissioners and the Department of the Environment, together with a share of the net proceeds of sale of redundant churches and sites. The provision is agreed on a five yearly basis and currently for the period 1 April 1979 to 31 March 1984 amounts to a maximum of £2,900,000. In addition the Fund as a charity may finance part of its expenditure by means of public appeals and is empowered to receive bequests and donations. The Fund consists of a Chairman and between four and six members all of whom are appointed by the Queen on the advice of the Archbishops of Canterbury and York submitted through the Prime Minister. As at 1st February 1980 148 redundant churches in England were vested in the Fund including the three Essex churches of *Chickney, East Horndon* and *West Bergholt*.

Under the Pastoral Measure the decision whether to vest a redundant church in the

95b. *West Bergholt. West gallery.*

95a. *East Horndon. Interior looking east.*

Fund, to put it to an alternative use or demolish it rests solely with the Church Commissioners. Unfortunately, their apparent unwillingness to vest in the Fund churches which are considered by many to be more than worthy of being vested sometimes provokes criticism. Two churches in Essex, *Mundon*, with its remarkable aisled belfry and *Wickham Bishops Old Church*, although not passed to the Fund were, however, leased to the Friends of Friendless Churches for appropriation as historic monuments. This body was set up in 1957 to help to preserve neglected churches and chapels as part of the nations' cultural heritage, irrespective of Pastoral considerations. The Friends currently own or lease sixteen churches in England and Wales.

Alternative uses

In its Annual Report for 1975 the Advisory Board for Redundant Churches stressed the importance of finding suitable uses for the maximum number of redundant churches to avoid both losing churches which deserve to be kept and overburdening the Redundant Churches Fund. It is generally accepted that the most successful conversions have been to educational, cultural and community use. *Colchester,* with eight churches of medieval origin within its central area, provides several interesting examples. *Holy Trinity* and *All Saints* have been acquired by the Borough Council for use as museums. *St Mary-at-the-Walls* and *St Martin* are both used for the performing arts, the former also being leased to the Borough Council. More controversially, *St Giles*, since redundancy used by the St John Ambulance Brigade, has since 1976 become a Masonic Hall. At *Asheldham* and *Witham All Saints,* Youth Centres have been established whilst *Plaistow, St Andrew* is used for community relations work.

Since the Pastoral Measure a number of Anglican churches have been taken over by other Christian denominations. *Leyton, St Edward* has been sold to the Elim Pentecostal Church whilst *Tolleshunt Knights* has been vested in the Greek Orthodox Church. Different and greater problems arise with non-Christian religions and sects.

In any conversion the criteria for suitability must remain the architectural or historic qualities of the rendundant church. Controversy is most aroused by proposals for the conversion of churches to residential use. The Advisory Board has emphasised the desirability of minimal structural alteration and that an open-plan galleried studio, as at *Langdon Hills,* is preferable to attempts to create as many rooms as possible on two floors with the need for additional light at an upper level. The obtrusive dormer windows at *Latchingdon, St Michael* emphasise the problem in this respect. At Latchingdon the Redundancy Scheme appropriating the church to residential use was brought in against strong local resistance. Essex County Council then rejected a planning application for conversion to a dwelling which was, however, subsequently reversed by the Secretary of State on appeal. The Friends of Friendless Churches has campaigned vigorously against conversions to residential use and the view that such conversion is putting a church to a "common or profane use" notwithstanding the oath given at its consecration is one that many Christians share. However, the Advisory Board and many Diocesan Redundant Churches Uses Committees regard the principle as quite acceptable. Other examples of local conversions to residential use may be found at *Shellow Bowells, Little Oakley* and *Frating.*

The future in Essex

Whilst it is impossible to predict the future flow of redundancies in the country as a whole it is to be hoped that the degree of rationalisation so far achieved in Essex by the working of the Pastoral Measure will have dealt with some of the most intractable problems. The introduction of State Aid to historic churches in use in 1978/9, the work of bodies like the *Essex Churches Support Trust* and the *Friends of Essex Churches* together with a growing public awareness of the great legacy that our parish churches represent, may well provide sufficient inspiration to enable many churches to be saved which would otherwise be lost to parochial use. Where a redundancy is necessary it is to be hoped that co-operation and goodwill between all interested parties will enable the church to be either preserved or appropriated to a use consistent with its past dignity, from which state in the fullness of time it may be brought back into parochial use again.

Epilogue

The Rt Revd John Trillo, Bishop of Chelmsford.

I have found this book absolutely fascinating and completely absorbing. It will certainly be my vade mecum as I travel around this vast diocese with its 660 churches, most of them medieval.

Our churches are unique, representing a veritable treasure house and throwing light on the history of our land and the ways of its people, rich and poor. Here all the arts and crafts of generations of men and women have been richly executed and displayed to the greater glory of God and to the edification of his people who have learned through eye as well as ear the good news of the Kingdom of God.

Well does Mr Laurence King write that "first and foremost we need to remember that our churches have been built for the honour and glory of God, where the Creator, Redeemer and Sanctifier of mankind may be worshipped by his people."

I have often been struck by prints of the eighteenth and nineteenth centuries which depict village churches as dilapidated and even ruinous. I believe that by comparison our churches are nowadays by and large infinitely better preserved and protected. Churchmen are very aware of the rare privilege which belongs to us as custodians and users of these buildings. I am only too well aware of the immense burden this places on congregations particularly in remote villages. Great sums of money are raised by efforts of whole villages on the part of churchmen and other well wishers. And grateful too that at last the Government makes grants to stimulate local generosity. This help is still modest considering the number of churches there are, but it is very welcome.

I am also grateful to the various agencies which provide help and advice to assist local congregations when they run into difficulty and among these I mention the Essex Churches Support Trust in particular. This Trust was founded two years ago after an initiative by the Lord Lieutenant at the time, Sir John Ruggles-Brise, and myself. It has quickly found its feet and produced a great deal of helpful material. It works closely with the Essex Churches Fund which makes grants where necessary.

We have all entered into a rich heritage of the Faith we hold and the churches where we worship. It is a trust we must ourselves enrich by our own Christian living and by an embellishment of all that is worthy in our buildings.

THE CONTRIBUTORS

Nancy Briggs, F.S.A.
Senior Assistant Archivist, Essex Record Office. Vice-President, Monumental Brass Society.

Peter Came, F.R.G.S.
Master at the Plume School, Maldon. For over 30 years a campanologist. Researcher and lecturer in local history and geography.

A. C. Edwards.
Formerly Lecturer, Essex Record Office, and County History Advisor. Author of *A History of Essex* and other books on local history.

Peter C. E. Elers.
Vicar of Thaxted. Member of the General Synod and of Chelmsford Diocesan Advisory Committee for the Care of Churches.

F. G. Emmison, M.B.E., F.S.A., F.R.Hist.S.
Former County Archivist. Author of *Elizabethan Life* (5 vols.)

William Grosvenor.
Administrator, Housing Corporation Headquarters. Chairman of Brentwood Civic Society and the All Saints Society which cares for East Horndon Church.

C. Harrold, C.Chem., F.R.S.C.
Manager. Author of *Discovering Thurrock* and contributor of the *County of Essex* for *Hatchments in Britain*.

C. A. Hewett.
Senior Officer, Historic Buildings and Conservation Section, Essex County Council. Author of *English Historic Carpentry* and other works.

Laurence King, O.B.E., F.S.A., F.R.I.B.A.
Architect. Member of Council for Places of Worship; Diocesan Advisory Committee, Southwark.

Rosemary Pardoe.
Writer and publisher of numerous works on Royal Heraldry in churches.

Warwick Rodwell, F.S.A.
Archaeologist and architectural historian. Initiated and directed archaeological studies of several Essex churches and a countywide survey. Author of many articles.

Anthony Russell, A.R.C.M., L.L.C.M., A.Mus.L.C.M., C.M.B.H.I.
Head of Music at the Plume School, Maldon.

Gillian Ward Russell, F.R.C.O., L.R.A.M., A.R.C.M., L.T.C.L.
Recitalist. Organist at Coggeshall church.

Christopher Starr.
Senior Personnel Officer, Housing Corporation Headquarters. Member of Chelmsford Diocesan Redundant Churches Uses Committee and Essex Churches Support Trust.

D. F. Stenning, Dipl. Arch.
Principal Planning Assistant, Essex County Planning Department.

ACKNOWLEDGEMENTS

The editor wishes to express his warmest thanks to the Suffolk Historic Churches Trust whose "Suffolk Churches, a pocket guide", was the model for this work: the contributors to the "Guide to Essex Churches" and the Committee of the Essex Churches Support Trust for their valuable help, advice and encouragement. Also to his wife Barbara Starr for typing and collating the numerous manuscript drafts of this book.

For the illustrations, grateful thanks to Victor Gray, County Archivist, for his permission to use material from the Essex Record Office 44.60.62.65a.72.75.76b. Gordon Ager 15.16.47b. Mark and Maidie Arman 25. C. A. Brooks Frontispiece. Christopher Dalton and the Redundant Churches Fund 93.95. A. C. Edwards 76a. C. Harrold 67c. Rosemary Pardoe 70.71. Warwick Rodwell 47a. Gillian Ward Russell and Anthony Russell 90. D.F. Stenning 32a.34. The remaining photographs are by Christopher Starr. Figure 1. Warwick Rodwell; figure 2. Victor Gray; figures 3.4.5.6.7. Nancy Briggs; figures 8.9. Christopher Starr; figures 10.11.12.13.14.15.16. Peter Came. The endpaper map is reprinted by permission of Penguin Books Ltd.

It is very much regretted that lack of space prevents the inclusion of a bibliography and glossary in this edition.

INDEX TO CHURCHES

Map references in **bold** type are to be read on the end paper map grid. Page numbers in *italic* are of illustrations.